EDUCATION, PHYSICAL EDUCATION
AND
PERSONALITY DEVELOPMENT

Education
Physical Education
and
Personality Development

by
P. J. ARNOLD, M.Ed.

Senior Lecturer in Education
and Physical Education,
Chelsea College, Eastbourne

HEINEMANN · LONDON

Heinemann Educational Books Ltd

LONDON EDINBURGH MELBOURNE AUCKLAND TORONTO
HONG KONG SINGAPORE KUALA LUMPUR NEW DELHI
NAIROBI JOHANNESBURG LUSAKA IBADAN
KINGSTON

ISBN 0 435 80035 3

© P. J. Arnold 1968
First published 1968
Reprinted 1970, 1972, 1976

Published by Heinemann Educational Books Ltd
48 Charles Street, London W1X 8AH
Printed in Great Britain by
Morrison and Gibb Ltd
London and Edinburgh

CONTENTS

v

FOREWORD

By the Rt. Hon. Philip Noel-Baker, M.P.
President of the International Council of Sport and Physical Education

Governments, universities, the leading writers, the world press have all begun to recognise the vast importance of physical recreation in the modern societies of the civilised world. Sport in all its many forms—games, track and field athletics, rowing, swimming, gymnastics, fencing, mountaineering, ski-ing, skating and the rest—have become a matter of daily and absorbing interest to hundreds of millions of people throughout the world. The Olympic Games have become incomparably the most successful international festival of any kind and perhaps the most hopeful for the future of man. The World Cup in Association Football, Wimbledon and other similar events, the Regional Games—European, Pan-American, Asian, African—rank only second to the Olympic Games themselves.

Not many people realise what a vast expansion of constructive international co-operation this world-wide growth of sport has brought about. In every major form of physical recreation there is now an International Federation, set up by democratic processes acting in accordance with accepted constitutional law, providing rules and regulations for the conduct of its sport throughout the world. This is a development of world institutions and of world law of vast significance. The occasional bad-tempered football match should not be allowed to obscure the fact that the laws of sport are faithfully observed in many tens of thousands of national, international, regional and world competitions every year.

No-one can doubt the great social importance of these developments. The leaders of sport hope that they will bring the practise of physical recreation within the grasp of every man and woman, boy and girl in all the Continents. The General Conference of U.N.E.S.C.O. last year instructed the Director General to prepare a programme for the action which the Governments could take to promote this end.

But at the basis of the growth of sport and physical recreation lies the vital factor of physical education in the schools and in the universities of the world. It is this subject which Mr. Peter Arnold treats in his most valuable work. He brings to his task not only great learning—his book bibliography alone shows how much research he has accomplished—but also practical experience of a very successful kind. He has been an outstanding physical educator himself, and his results commend his book to the attention of all those who are concerned with educational work. The Ancient Greeks knew, and we are learning, that physical recreation is a vitally important part of the education of the 'balanced' man.

Mr. Arnold has made a notable contribution to thought on this subject and I warmly commend his book to all readers who are interested in the theme with which it deals.

London, November 1967.   PHILIP J. NOEL-BAKER

ACKNOWLEDGMENTS

IT WOULD be impossible to name the innumerable people with whom I have worked, discussed and clarified my thoughts. To all these friends, colleagues and acquaintances I am indebted. At the manuscript stage I would like to thank particularly Mr. R. M. Wight and Mr. J. Bradley, both of Leicester University School of Education, for their valuable comments and suggestions. Needless to say for any opinions expressed, judgements made or errors uncorrected I alone am responsible. In addition my thanks must go to Lynda Black and Marian Pudge for helping to arrange the indexes. Also to Rita Arkley, librarian at Chelsea College, for reading through the final proofs. Lastly, I am indebted to Christine Brown, whose efficient typing and generous assistance throughout the entire undertaking was of immense help.

P. J. ARNOLD

INTRODUCTION

Physical education can be defined as that integral part of the educational process which enhances and harmonises the physical, intellectual, social and emotional aspects of an individual's personality chiefly through directed physical activity. Thus it has an obvious importance in the development of personality itself. Eysenck [1], for example, offers the following definition: 'Personality is the more or less stable and enduring organisation of a person's character, temperament, intellect and physique, which determines his unique adjustment to the environment'. The phrase 'more or less' here is all important for without it there would be little room for the educational process to operate. Eysenck goes on to associate character with *will* or conative behaviour; temperament with *emotion* or affective behaviour; intellect with *intelligence* or cognitive behaviour; and physique with bodily configuration and neuro-endocrine endowment. The area with which physical education deals is similar to the regions covered by the term personality. In fact it aims to affect and modify advantageously the development of personality through the medium of physical activity. Whereas personality is a state of *being*, physical education is a process of *doing*.

It is the aim in the chapters that follow to discuss at some length how it is that physical or activity education can contribute something to the creation of healthy personalities and full living.

The role of play throughout the period of growth is of paramount importance in the development of the child. It may seem at first sight that what has been said of physical education might with equal truth be said of play. Each, it is true, has a great deal in common with the other, so much so in fact that it became necessary to insert the word 'directed' in our definition in order to bring about an undoubted distinction between them.* Play may be regarded as coming within the scope of

* For a more detailed analysis of play and physical education differences consult P. J. Arnold's article, 'Leisure, Recreation, Play and Physical Education', in University of London Institute of Education's *Bulletin*. New Series, No 11, Spring Term, 1967, pp. 25-7.

physical education but it is not an interchangeable term. Play and physical education differ in three main ways. Whereas play tends to be spontaneous, physical education tends to require deliberation in thought and practice; whereas play is directed to no particular overall ends, physical education is directed towards the main-stream of general educational endeavour; whereas play is essentially an expression of uninhibited absorption, physical education may sometimes reflect an attitude of disciplined application. The degree of shift that occurs between these two psychological poles determines whether the child is at play or work. It is, of course, the aim of the physical educationist to promote his programme in such a way that he will generate a play spirit. That this does not always come about does not mean that he has failed. It does not necessarily mean either that from the educational point of view the experience is less rewarding. Some worthwhile activities, swimming for example, can only be learnt when the learner is aware of his own conscious effort. Since both play and physical education will be terms used a good deal in the discussions that follow, it is as well that we have in our minds a clear idea of their differences.

While a good deal will be spoken on behalf of physical education, it has not been overlooked that learning and the manner of it depends largely upon the teacher. For the purposes of this book the term teacher applies both to the ordinary parent and the trained professional.

The form of the book requires perhaps a brief explanation. The introductory chapter propounds the desirability for balance in life and synthesis in learning experience. It goes on to suggest, after a critique of current dangers, that physical education has a distinctive part to play in this worthwhile endeavour. The main body of the text explains what contribution the physical element in education can make to the overall development of the personality with reference to the periods of infancy, childhood and adolescence. This is done by examining how, with enlightened guidance, the subject can advantageously affect the physical, mental, emotional and social aspects of the personality and through them assist many of the educative processes.

The last chapter relates back to the first and shows that what has been argued with reference to the growing individual is largely applicable when the needs of society itself are diagnosed.

CHAPTER ONE

THE THEORETICAL AND SOCIAL FRAMEWORK OF PHYSICAL EDUCATION

Balance—the Greek Ideal

It was in the age of the classical Greeks that the idea of balance in life was first extolled. By balance they meant the harmonious development of the physical, mental and spiritual aspects of man through which the unity of the soul was to be achieved. This philosophic ideal is recorded in the writings of Pythagoras [2] and Plato [3]. Its most perfect exemplification is perhaps found in fifth-century B.C. Athens when in all fields of endeavour men of genius sprang up in such profusion. The Spartan, who emphasised the body, and the ascetic of the Middle Ages, who emphasised the spirit, both lived lives of imbalance. When, today, Jacks [4] talks about the education of the whole man and Jeffreys [5] talks about the need for a 'coherent view of life' they are both re-affirming a belief in the Greek ideal of balance. Concepts arising from modern scientific studies of mankind seem to underline and substantiate its importance. The physiologist, for example, speaks of homeostasis, the developmental psychologist of equilibrium, the psychiatrist of integrated personality. When Schweitzer's [6] ethic of reverence for life is examined carefully, we come to see that this too involves balance—a balance of values by which one individual can live successfully with another.

Dewey's Theory of 'Experiential Continuum'

In our approach to democratic education we approve of almost all of these ideas to do with balance in theory. It is not the idea of balance about which there is disagreement amongst educational philosophers so much as the means of bringing it about. In the writings of Dewey [7] we find the most complete answer to this problem. In his *Education and Experience* he propounds a theory of experiential continuum which maintains that every experience both takes up something from those which have gone before and modifies in some way the quality of those

3

which come after. Since he contends that democratic social arrangements promote a better quality of human experience than non-democratic or anti-democratic forms of social life, education, which is 'planned experience', can best be served by being conducted in such a milieu. The quality of experience, then, is his justification for a democratic approach to education. But what does he mean by quality of experience? He means that a child's education should be on-going and integrative. Physical, intellectual, emotional and social aspects of his development should be synthesised—his personal development should be balanced against that of his social development. The cultivation of an individual's faculties in a social setting and with a social responsibility was Dewey's aim.

He interprets his theory with the aid of two principles. The first is the principle of continuity, one exemplification of which is found in the concept of growth. Experiences as they are presented to the child should be on-going. Aspects of development should be educative in the sense that they unite and lead on to further development. Maturity should accompany growth and bring about greater understanding and greater sociability in contact and communication. Education, he implies, must be understood in terms of the child's growth and development, if the theory is to be successful. Interaction expresses the second principle for looking at an experience in its dynamic state. It assigns equal rights in both factors of experience—the objective and the subjective. The former is concerned with the environmental conditions and the external stimuli. The situation is the precise environment, e.g. learning how to swim. The latter is concerned with the personal reactions of the pupil, e.g. apprehension about putting his head under the water. Educative experience must take account of both these factors. Experiences can sometimes, however, be mis-educative if the one does not take sufficient notice of the other. If, for example, in teaching a child how to swim the teacher is unsympathetic to the child's fear and, in an effort to get the child to put his head under the water, ducks him, the experience for the child would be mis-educative. It would increase his fear of the water, upset his relationship with the teacher, and impede, if not destroy, his progress at swimming. Not all experiences then are on-going and educative. To avoid these mis-educative experiences and ensure the onward growth of the personality, the teacher should not only take care in the progressive selection of activities (environmental or extrinsic factor) but do the same in the handling of the child's mind (subjective or intrinsic factor). Only by enlightened attention to both these factors can the teacher lead the child to higher levels of integration and maturity.

Values, attitudes and standards are all a part of our experiential continuum and how physical education can contribute to their harmonisation and development as a part of the total educational process is the subiect of later chapters. In the meantime we must concern ourselves more with the disparities that have arisen between the theoretical exposition of Dewey's ideas and the practical application of them.

Application and Synthesis
Dewey's pedagogical writings have come to dominate the educational scene in the U.S.A. His influence there has been profound. In this country his ideas began to receive attention in the years between the World Wars and are unmistakably represented in the Hadow Reports on Primary and Secondary education that were published in this period.

His desire to 'psychologise' the curriculum and relate one piece of knowledge to another was a reaction against the departmentalised approach of the old system of teaching with its artificial division of subjects. The child, he pointed out, was at the centre of the educational process—not the subject matter —and consequently teaching should be based upon his interests, activities and needs. This demand for a re-orientation of thought was not immediately successful and it took several years before the ways of the 'New' education replaced the formalised methods of the 'Old'.

Unity and balance in experience was to come about by providing occupations that would utilise all the child's faculties. Activity became a key word. Activity to Dewey meant the engagement of the mind as well as of the body. The employment of both at the same time was desirable as by synthesising the experience of each with the other harmony and development could proceed together. The implications of this synthesising of experience are important. All elements in education, it will be seen, will interact with one another and thus affect one another. Since the physical element no less than the mental or spiritual element is open to educative or mis-educative experience the educationist must see that each element plays its part in an educative and fruitful manner, if the education of the child is to proceed on sound and wholesome lines.

If one of these elements is neglected or over-emphasised the result is likely to lead to experiential imbalance and to a distorted growth of the personality. It would seem to follow therefore that good education not only involves a proportionate balance between the elements but as much interaction of them as is possible so that one form of experience merges with another in a pool of synthesised experience. Such an achievement should manifest itself in the ability to see relationships and in healthy personality adjustment.

Although, in general, recognition is given to Dewey's main principles, it would appear that education today is in danger of failing to meet them on two counts. Firstly, there is a growing tendency to imbalance between the three elements. Secondly, the gap in the studied relationship of one subject to another is widening. These two processes are occurring despite ourselves. The reasons for this increasing disparity between what is advocated and what is done we shall examine with particular reference to the position of physical education.

Theory and Practice Today

In nearly all educational institutions great play is made of phrases like transfer of the effects of training, integration of subjects, organismic approach, cross fertilisation, general education and liberal education. They are presented with the idea of enlivening and equipping the minds of the forthcoming generation of teachers so that theory can be transmitted into practice. Fragmentation of knowledge and lop-sided development are condemned. Despite this clear advocacy, which is well in accord with Dewey's theory, the practical effects are disappointing. When does the difficulty start?

Most of these aids to teaching are in ample evidence throughout the years of the Nursery School but from then on the process of segregation and differentiation sets in. The work of the last year or two of the Primary School leads to some form of Secondary School selection and from this point on each piece of knowledge is in danger of being confined to the subject with which it is directly concerned. Formality replaces the freedom of play and first-hand experiential learning. The organism rarely becomes totally involved—only bits of it are appealed to at a time. The areas of prepared knowledge are catered for in neat categorised slices. In the Secondary Schools education is often reduced to a question of timetable administration. In some Grammar Schools this in turn is subjected to the exigencies of examination requirements. Examinations and their paralysing impact, especially amongst the senior forms of our Secondary Schools, have virtually destroyed the prospect of a liberal education. While the passing of examinations may come to be regarded as an inevitable part of our educational system it should not necessarily mean that those aspects of education that are not examined should be squeezed out of existence. Indeed, there is every good reason to keep them if proportion and balance are to be maintained. Physical education, along with other non-examined subjects, has a real justification for inclusion in a programme which lays claims to total education. Any programme which cuts across the unification of the growth process is in danger of distorting the balanced development of the individual. The teachers themselves may be aware of such dangers, but as victims of the machinations of a system they can do little about it. Education today suffers from the sad dichotomy of having an educational theory that is essentially sound, but which is difficult to put into practical effect because of the pernicious examination system imposed upon it. This is particularly true in the Grammar Schools and Comprehensive education, for the intellectually able, promises to fare no better in this respect. The long-term effects of this dichotomy are not easy to pin-point but it would appear that in the minds of the pupils, if not in those of their teachers, there exists a series of dualisms—between the value of examined and non-examined subjects and between the intellectual and the physical. Although not closely related to examinations there is the further dualism between the morality of Christian ethics and behaviour as they see it about them. Symptoms like these indicate a lack of harmony in education. The state of affairs exists and is not easily alterable; yet something ought to be done and can be done. Until such time as a major overhaul comes about the prime responsibility for balance and synthesis must remain in the hands of the individual teacher. Since the teacher of an examined subject is largely a slave of his syllabus the real opportunity must lie with teachers of non-examined subjects. Here the physical educationist can help to rectify the imbalance and lack of synthesis.

Physical education is a subject and yet more than a subject. It is to do with skills, yet perhaps more important it is to do with the person. With its multifarious activities and possibilities it covers everything in education which is to do with the physical. In recent years many physical educationists have been at great pains to explain that they are concerned primarily with education *through* the physical rather than *of* the physical. The new concept introduced by the change in preposition has made the subject respectable in most schools and is now thought about in more comprehensive terms. Even physical education teachers sometimes glibly refer to its biological, psychological and social values without fully understanding their import. Indeed, these so-called principles operate as a shield behind which many give themselves intellectual protection. Their actual teaching, however, far from incorporating and applying them in an enlightened fashion, is characterised by the limitation of the question *how* rather than by the philosophic question *why*. For physical education teachers, whose minds are preoccupied by method and function, the reason *why* they are doing what they are doing must remain a puzzle. Their uncertainty of thought is ruthlessly exposed by their pupils who ask why it is that they have to 'waste time' with P.E. when they have pressing examination commitments ahead, or why they are doing this activity as opposed to that. To be able to give satisfactory answers to questions of this sort it is necessary for the teacher of physical education to have a *raison d'être* which is based upon a thought-out position of educational philosophy. Hackneyed phrases and cliches are not enough. They are often a cover for superficial and ill-equipped minds which are used but which lack direction and purpose. The physical educationist should at least go some way to resolving the first two of the dualisms mentioned. He has the philosophical concept of the body-mind; the findings of psychology, with its theories of learning and adjustment; and more recently he has that branch of medicine called psychosomatics to call upon. The unity of the organism and the interaction between its parts is confirmed in one research finding after another. Any system of education which denies this unity and impedes the synthesis of one element with another will, as we have seen, disturb the integration of the personality. Examinations with their narrow requirements have already made damaging incursions in this direction. It is up to the teachers of non-examined subjects who, unhampered by rigid syllabi, can counteract these forces of fragmentation.

The P.E. teacher can perhaps help in this endeavour more than any other for he alone is concerned with his pupils' bodies as well as their intellect, emotions and sociability, and because of this he has enormous educative scope. However the educational process is life-long and all-embracing and is therefore not confined to school age or school time. The wider sociological implications are important and the next section is devoted to a discussion of them.

Education and Society
Attention, so far, has been confined to education within the school situation and it has been shown how practice can run foul of theory. Compared to the world of adult society, however, the microcosm of the school leads a tolerably balanced existence. It touches, at least superficially, upon those aspects of integration and growth about which we have been speaking. Its members are introduced to intellectual matters by being acquainted with areas of knowledge; they share in a common act of worship and receive some religious instruction; they play games and take other forms of exercise that keep them physically active; they lead a social life by being in a community and by participating in its activities. Some degree of balance is at least evident on the timetable if not in effect. Even for pupils caught up in a pernicious examination system with its narrow specialisation, school life remains at least reasonably balanced. For the child who comes from an emotionally deprived and philistine home the school can be a haven of abundance and goodness. The school though, in common with other institutions, is not an island unto itself. It fits into and is a part of a larger social framework. Its influence, no matter how great, makes its impress along with other influences in the environment. In this moulding process the school, the home, the neighbourhood and the community at large all make their contributions to the developing personality. No matter how good the education is within a particular establishment, its effect is modified to some

extent by the nature of the environment in which it operates. As Pinion [8] succinctly reminds us: 'Whatever is claimed for organised education, whether in the schools, the universities or colleges of technology, the forces which contribute most to our culture and progress, or lack of progress, are at work outside', or in the words of Brameld [9], 'Education, broadly understood, is a fundamental agency of culture' and 'Education will be transformed no less thoroughly than the culture that sustains it and upon which it will exert an enormous influence'. If these assertions are true, it seems to follow that if education (used in its broadest sense) is to succeed and be 'on-going' and lead to 'growth', the aims and practices of schools and society must be in general accord. The one must be the complement of the other. Thus Jeffreys [10] speaks about the need for a 'coherent view' of life. We have only to look about us to see that this is not so at the present time. Before taking this point further let us first look at the condition of our society.

To the boy or girl who leaves school at fifteen even the theoretical balance of a timetable is no longer available. The school-leaver is pitched out into a pagan world of commercial practice and canned culture.* The adult world with which he is confronted is cynical of the sentiments and beliefs in which he had half his being and is ready to laugh at his innocence. Rather than be scorned he accepts the prevalent materialistic outlook and succumbs to the narcosis of mass media. Unlike his more intelligent Grammar School contemporary, who remains to some extent insulated from such pressures for a further year or two, he becomes an easy prey of the social milieu in which he finds himself. In short he becomes a victim of the society in which he lives, works and takes his leisure. The dangers and debilitating effects on the individual of being amorphously absorbed by a society without clearly recognised values are well described in the works of Durkheim [11] and Riesman [12].†

Just as an individual can become ill so too can a society. In

* A good account of the problems the adolescent has to face in transferring from school to work is given in M. Carter's *Into Work* (Penguin, 1966).

† Anomie is a term used by Durkheim to refer to the individual's loss of social cohesion—of shared sentiments and values. In the phrase 'other-directedness' Riesman expresses the increasing tendency of the individual in modern society to subordinate his own values to the expectations of others who surround him. Other-directedness reflects an impoverishment of the personality.

the progressive disintegration of the last one hundred and fifty years society has become gradually sick. Halliday [13] on examining the phenomenon of the 'sick society' makes the point that this is not due to a deterioration in physical health, which has in fact improved, but to the disintegrating effects of the pattern of modern life. The real psychological needs (as opposed to materialistic wants) of society, he maintains, are not being met. That there is evidence for such a conclusion is undeniable.

Sociologists, religious leaders, as well as psychiatrists are agreed that the social ailments that are affecting our society are becoming increasingly conspicuous. Figures for crime, delinquent acts, pre-marital pregnancy, alcoholism and divorce have all steadily worsened per 100,000 of the population since 1938 and the churches are probably emptier now than they have ever been. Epidemiologists are busy trying to account for the extension of such ill-defined illnesses as cardio-vascular disease, psychosomatic disorders and the psycho-neuroses whose causes have to be looked for in the individual and his habits rather than in the hostile attack by external organisms. As Carstairs [14] says, 'His behaviour, his diet, his mode of life and his personal relations may well play a part in their development'. Symptoms and statistics, if they are any-thing to go by, do seem to substantiate the idea that the condition of the nation, in common with other western com-munities, is sick. What causes can be found to explain the malaise of the West? The Industrial Revolution, now at an automated stage; the Welfare State with its accompanying rapid social changes; the decline of belief in traditional values have all been given as reasons. The existence of the hydrogen bomb, with its unprecedented powers of destruction, may also account for an unconscious anxiety. The European world probably feels more insecure now than at any time since the fall of the Roman Empire.

To these outer events, to which we may reasonably ascribe some of our ills, Fromm [15], probing beneath the surface, adds an inner event which is perhaps even more important. In his book *The Fear of Freedom* he describes the stages by which man has striven to throw off the yoke of medieval thought and gain his independence. Now that he has largely gained his freedom from a faith in God he remains fearful and alone. Spiritual desolation can be even more bewildering than the ascribable fear of a positive event. This is particularly true of the common person and may to some extent explain our current troubles. To quote Jung [16]: 'If dull people lose the idea of God nothing happens—not immediately and personally at least. But socially the masses begin to breed mental epidemics, of which we now have a fair number.'

What then is the answer for a society such as ours which is heterogeneous in its make-up, confused in its values and showing symptoms of social sickness? The educative process, it seems, is the only process which is sufficiently comprehensive to synthesise and attempt to make coherent the multifarious aspects of life that come to bear on the individual. The difficulties are immense. Always in a democratic society the individual rights of the person must be balanced against the social claims of the community. In these circumstances education must aim not only to develop each citizen maximally but to make each citizen aware of his responsibilities to other citizens. In our double-barrelled aim the results of the social factor as well as of the personal factor have been disappointingly apparent. In our brief survey of social sickness some of the raw spots have been touched upon. Education and educational policy should not dissociate themselves from these events but should be actively concerned with their prevention and alleviation. It is true that in response to a growing social consciousness the government has interested itself more in the solution of such problems. Through its active intervention a number of reports (Crowther, Albemarle, Wolfenden, Pilkington, Beloe, Newsom, Plowden) have been brought out and each has made observations and recommendations, some of which have been noted and acted upon, but helpful though these reports have been, their proposals do not bring a complete solution.

The raising of the school leaving age to sixteen, the introduction of a new examination, the provision of extra facilities, the training of youth leaders, the reduction of class sizes, the establishment of priority areas for redevelopment, envisaged by these reports may go some way to curing some of our young people's boredom and maladjustment. But unless their interests, habits and values can be cultivated before they leave school to a reasonably integrated and mature degree the next generation will be as gullible and as malleable to the pressures of mass media as the present one is. Regeneration, it is clear, must come from below and be nourished from above. The most ill-at-ease section of the community is the one that leaves school early and, until marriage, enters upon a period of frustration and ennui. It is right that the needs of these pre-adult young people should find wholesome and satisfying outlets. Everything should be done to encourage them into worthwhile pursuits but, unless they are convinced by the essential soundness and worthwhile-ness of them, the efforts now being made on their behalf may prove fruitless. The Crowther [17] report, for example, speaks of the youths who have access to clubs but remain outside them. It is generally true to say that only acceptable youths want to join clubs and these form a minority. The unclubbables are the real problem. It is frequently too late to persuade them after they have left school that their tastes are low, that their values are unsound and that their boredom springs more from their needs going unsatisfied rather than from an absence of entertainment.

If children can be interested in and awakened to the joy and balance of a well-adapted life when they are at school, they may more readily pass on to the Youth Centres, the Village Colleges and other places of further education, where they can redress some of the imbalance caused by a dull and routine occupation after they have left school. Industry, too, should do more than it does for young trainees. It should realise, as many welfare officers do, that the best adjusted people tend to make the best workers.

Many of the improvements so far discussed in Parliament and elsewhere, helpful and valuable though they are, will prove to be of no avail in meeting the real predicament of our society unless the educative process is one of quality. This essentially comprises a careful nurturing of all things that are good. We get a hint of how to go about this from Plato [18] but whereas he had his guardian class in mind, we in our society should bear in mind all classes in the community:

> We would not have our guardians grow up amongst representa-
> tions of moral deformity, as in some foul pasture where, day after
> day, feeding on every poisonous weed, they would, little by little,
> gather insensibly a mass of corruption in their very souls. Rather
> we must seek out for them those craftsmen whose instinct guides
> them to whatsoever is lovely and gracious; so that our young men,

dwelling in a wholesome climate, may drink in good from every quarter, whence, like a breeze bearing health from happy regions some influence from noble works constantly falls upon eye and ear from childhood upward, and imperceptibly draws them into sympathy and harmony with the beauty of reason, whose impress they take.

An idyll such as this may be impossible to attain, yet to strive towards it is no less a responsibility of those in authority in society than those who teach in the schools and those who are parents in the home. In a world which no longer subscribes to the binding force of Christian ethical teaching, educationists must look for other sources of good to which all teachers, no matter what their belief, can readily commit themselves. Just as they should work towards balance and integration in know-ledge, so too should they work towards a respect and reverence for human personality. Such a concept is well in accord with Schweitzer's ethic of a 'reverence for life' [19] to which reference has been made earlier. To give practical respect to personality involves the consideration of all its aspects so that they may be nurtured with a care and understanding that will in turn lead on not only to the welfare of the person but to the welfare of other people with whom he shares his life. The interests of both individual and society would thus be served. Education then, if it is to foster such an aim, should concern itself with the harmonisation of those areas of personality which the psychologists have shown to be crucial to a sound develop-ment. They are complexly interwoven but for convenience can be called the physical, the intellectual, the emotional and the social. Earlier we discussed them in somewhat abstract terms but these elements should manifest themselves in such observ-able attributes as health, curiosity, tolerance, aesthetic sensi-tivity, expressive creativity, and a consideration for others, if education in respect of personality is being conducted on enlightened and integrative lines. Working in such a manner the educationist can contribute something towards the coher-ence which our society so badly needs. In this momentous endeavour physical education will have its part to play. By educating *by*, *through* and *of* the physical, physical education touches upon all those aspects of personality that lead to a wholesome and well-conducted life. We must now turn to a consideration of how best this can be done up to the age of eighteen. Before doing so, however, the words of Lewis Mumford are worth recalling [20]:

> In attempting to restore balance in the community and in the personality, we need not be troubled by references to the undoubted existence of individual differences or to the fact, as true in society as in the human organism, that all equilibrium is necessarily unstable and is constantly upset by the continued act of growth. The first condition makes the effort to achieve a fuller and more balanced development necessary: the second makes it an ideal goal—one always to be aimed at but never, in the nature of things, fully achieved.

BOOKS FOR FURTHER READING

Bowra, C. M., *The Greek Experience*. Mentor, 1964.

Carstairs, G. M., *This Island Now*. Penguin, 1964.

Carter, M., *Into Work*. Penguin, 1966.

Dewey, J., *Experience and Education*. N.Y. Macmillan, 1946.

—— *Democracy and Education*. N.Y. Macmillan, 1916.

Elvin, H. L., *Education and Contemporary Society*. Watts, 1965.

Eysenck, H. J., *The Structure of Human Personality*. Methuen, 1960.

Fyvel, T. R., *The Insecure Offenders*. Penguin, 1963.

Jeffreys, M. V. C., *Personal Values in the Modern World*. Penguin, 1962.

Morse, M., *The Unattached*. Penguin, 1965.

Pinion, F. B., *Educational Values in an Age of Technology*. Maxwell, 1964.

Plato, *Republic* (Translated by F. M. Cornford). Clarendon Press, Oxford, 1941.

Riesman, D., *The Lonely Crowd*. Yale University Press, 1950.

The Albemarle Report (The Youth Service in England and Wales). H.M.S.O., 1960.

The Crowther Report (15 to 18). H.M.S.O., 1959.

The Newsom Report (Half Our Future). H.M.S.O., 1963.

The Plowden Report (Children and their Primary Schools). H.M.S.O., 1966.

CHAPTER TWO

THE PHYSICAL ELEMENT IN PHYSICAL EDUCATION

THE BIOLOGICAL BASIS OF PHYSICAL EDUCATION

Introduction

It is commonly agreed by developmental psychologists that throughout the period of growth there is within the human system an inner drive for activity. At different stages of growth activity is characteristically expressed in accordance with intrinsic biological laws. The job of the physical educationist is to have a working understanding of these laws so that he may modify their natural course and direct them towards the functional skills and values which are in keeping with our general educational striving. In doing so he should remember that his is the work of the gardener rather than the builder and that his influence whether in the gymnasium, swimming pool or classroom is always being transmitted through the process of interaction. He should remember too that each pupil has a mind as well as a body and that growth and development manifest advances on both fronts. The interrelatedness and interdependence of the two reflects itself in the physical, intellectual, emotional and social aspects of our living and this he should remember also. The child according to Gesell [21] is a 'unitary action system' and his emerging personality should always be looked at against the background of his total situation. The child is more than the sum total of his parts. It is more in the integral make-up of the parts that an understanding of the 'holistic' nature of the child will come. As Goldstein [22] has observed: 'A specific performance . . . is a specific pattern of the whole organism. . . . Each stimulation always causes a change in the entire condition, and only apparently a locally confined change.'

Confronted with the intricate complexity of child behaviour, the physical educationist should approach the task of understanding with deference and due humility. In the teaching of a simple skill, for example, he should attempt to guage the individual learning potential of the pupil; his emotional re-action as an aid and as a deterrent; his regard of it as function-ally useful and socially important. Only after an all round look at the child will the physical educationist be able to see how circumstances can be altered to produce a successful piece of teaching or a successful programme of work.

The Concept of Health

The time honoured maxim of *mens sana in corpore sano* implies that health is more than an absence of disease, and so it is. Health should be regarded more as a positive concept than a negative one. It should involve not only the efficient functioning of the bodily machine, but playing one's part in the full richness of living. Something of the comprehensiveness that is attendant on the meaning of the term is conveyed in the World Health Organisation's definition which states that, 'health is a state of complete physical, mental and social well-being and not merely the absence of disease and infirmity'. Such a definition does not necessarily mean that a healthy person always passes through life harmoniously and without discord. Rather it suggests that one's personality aspects and powers are acting in an integrated fashion. Thomson [23] expresses the position in these words:

> The healthy man has a wholeness or oneness of physical life while the unhealthy man is always distracted. And though the healthy man may be torn by temptations and puzzled by the unsolved problems of life, he has not often to fight a battle on two fronts, for health implies some degree of unity. The unhealthy man on the other hand, has always to face bodily discord as well as ethical and intellectual difficulties. He is not at peace with his own body.

It becomes clear, if the above quotation is true, that health can only be conceived in holistic or psychosomatic terms. Since physical education is to do with the mind as well as the body in the form of the person, the question of health is a subject of real importance. That there is a connection between the state of the mind and the state of the body is now undoubted. It is shown more clearly perhaps when the person is in a condition of illness. Mohr [24] puts the matter this way: 'There is no such thing as a purely psychic illness or a purely physical illness, but only a "living event" taking place in a living organism which is itself alive only by virtue of the fact that in it psychic and somatic are united in a unity'. This two-way process of the mind affecting the body and the body affecting the mind is of vital interest to the physical educationist for it does indicate that the state of the organism is an important aspect of health. By keeping the bodily organs in a fit and functional state there is less likelihood of them distracting the mind from its work. Organic fitness may even help concentration and intellectual perseverance. More certain is the fact that organic fitness is a sound basis from which to learn motor skills and to participate successfully in physical activities, both of which have been experimentally shown to be closely related to problems of adjustment and therefore to the mental aspect of health [25 and 26]. At all events organic fitness may be regarded as an integral part of total health and it is the responsibility of physical educationists to administer and promote a programme that will bring it about.

Health, Adjustment and Academic Achievement
Before we go on to examine how organic fitness can be brought about and what its particular effects are, let us first note a number of findings which show a connection between health and academic performance.

Of the many studies to do with gifted children two are outstanding. These are by Witty [27] and Terman [28]. The general conclusion of both is that the gifted child is generally above the average in physical health and strength. In answer to the question, 'In what respects does the typical gifted child differ from the typical child of normal mentality?' Terman and Oden found some interesting relationships. The first was that schoolchildren representative of the top 1% of tested intelligence are, as a group, superior in other respects as well. They rate far above the average in physique, social adjustment, personality traits, school achievement, play information, and versatility of interests. Secondly, from childhood to maturity the gifted have continued to rate above the average in health. On this matter they report:

> The results of the physical measurements and the medical examinations provide a striking contrast to the popular stereotype of the child prodigy, so commonly predicted as a pathetic creature, over-serious, undersized, sickly, hollow-chested, nervously tense

and bespectacled. There are gifted children who bear some resemblance to this stereotype, but the truth is that almost every element in the picture, except the last, is less characteristic of the gifted child than of the mentally average.

Two other studies show a converse relationship. Page [29] found at Syracuse University that 83% of the male students dismissed at the end of their first year for poor academic achievements had Physical Fitness Indices below 100; 39% had P.F.I.s below 85. A similar pattern is presented by Coelfield and McCollum [30] who at the University of Oregon in 1954 found that 78 male freshmen with the lowest P.F.I.s were also below average in academic accomplishment when compared to their contemporaries. The significant point about these findings is not so much in the fact that below average P.F.I. scores related to below average scholastic achievement but in the knowledge that in both studies the known scholastic aptitude scores were above average.

It would be unwise to draw too hasty conclusions from these studies showing the relationship between organic fitness and academic achievement as evidence is still relatively limited. At the same time, however, such evidence as there is suggests that on the one hand there is a relationship between above average health, adjustment and exceptional academic achievement and on the other hand a relationship between low organic fitness and low scholastic achievement even when potential ability was above average. Findings such as the ones cited give support to Garrison's [31] statement that, 'A sound physical condition and abundant health are basic foundations for a well-adjusted and completely integrated life'.

Organic Fitness and Physical Education
Reference has already been made to organic fitness as an integral part of the concept of health. It is one of the prime tasks of physical education to see that the organic state of the body is kept in good repair and to enhance its functional efficiency. If it does so effectively physical education can justifiably claim to be making a real contribution to furthering the health of the emerging personality.

One of the fundamental laws in physiology is that the functional efficiency of an organism improves with use and regresses with disuse. Accordingly, it follows that if the human machine is to be kept in good working order some exercise is necessary. Leaving aside concomitant considerations such as age, nutrition and disease let us look at the effect of vigorous activity on the bodily systems.

SKELETO-MUSCULAR SYSTEM. Sustained vigorous exercise affects both muscles and bones. Muscle fibres increase in size and the number of blood capillaries supplying them increases. This joint result has three main advantages. Firstly, there is a gain in strength owing to the ability to produce more powerful contractions. Secondly, there is an increase in speed because of the ability to repeat contractions more rapidly. Thirdly, there is a gain in endurance as a result of an improved capillary supply and consequent oxygen availability. There is some evidence [32 and 33] to suggest that exercise helps in the sufficient supply of calcium which is so necessary to satisfactory bone formation. Certainly the converse is true: that inactivity results in the depletion of the normal stores of both calcium and protein.

NEURO-MUSCULAR SYSTEM. Another effect of 'educated' muscle action is reflected in the efficiency with which the muscles are used. Exercise, intelligently taken, should lead to an improvement in both precision and economy. It has been found [34], for example, that a co-ordinated movement can save by as much as up to a quarter in terms of energy loss over a movement that is executed clumsily and in an unco-ordinated manner. We shall talk more about this when we come to consider the development of motor skills.

CARDIO-VASCULAR SYSTEM. With vigorous exercise the heart becomes larger and more efficient and is able to circulate more blood whilst beating less frequently. This increased efficiency of the heart enables a larger flow to reach the muscles thus ensuring an improved supply of fuel and oxygen so that the organism can withstand a greater amount of work. One other effect of vigorous exercise is that it leads to a reduction in the amount of time it takes the body to recover after strenuous activity. It is the opinion of many medical practitioners that there is a close correlation between the sedentary, push-button character of our culture and the constantly rising incidence of coronary artery disease and other forms of cardio-vascular disturbance. A reflection by Mellerowicz [35] is perhaps not out of place here. He said that 'domestication and civilisation bring about an economy deficit of the circulatory system. This leads to a continuous over-demand with premature degenerative lesions and clearly aging phenomena of the circulatory system. The small "normal" heart of the con-temporary domesticated and civilised man, when compared to the heart of an athlete, seems to be morphologically degenerated and functionally inferior. . . .' A comment such as this only re-inforces the view that the effect of exercise on organic fitness not only acts as a form of preventive medicine but gives a reserve of vitality that can be called upon without detriment to the organism in cases of emergency.

THE RESPIRATORY SYSTEM. Exercise increases the demand for oxygen and thus causes an increase in respiratory activity. A person who has indulged in regular exercise has a number of advantages over an inactive person. Firstly, the respiratory muscles—the diaphragm, the stomach and thoracic muscles—all improve in efficiency. Secondly, a greater proportion of the lung area is accessible to air. This means that he has a greater capacity for getting oxygen to the tissues. Thirdly, he is able to absorb a greater percentage of oxygen from the amount that is breathed. Again there is a greater reserve capacity for full and active living.

THE DIGESTIVE SYSTEM. The advantages of exercise on the digestive system are twofold. Firstly, the chemical action is assisted by the increased circulation of the blood and the movement of the abdominal muscles. Secondly, the peristaltic action of the alimentary canal and intestines is improved as a result of good muscle tone.

THE EXCRETORY SYSTEM. The excretory system is kept in good functioning order as a result of exercise in two main ways. In the first place increased abdominal strength and increased blood circulation help with efficient elimination. In the second place the possibility of overburdening the kidneys in their proper discharge of waste fluids is reduced since exercise acts to some extent as an excess weight control. Constipation or the inefficient discharge of waste produce can lead to a variety of ailments including headaches, pains and a feeling of general debility.

Ways of promoting organic fitness in Physical Education
One of the first responsibilities of physical education is to bring about a state of organic fitness. This can be accomplished by hard and sustained exercise. The various activities that comprise the trained physical educationist's programme are particularly suited to do this. An increase in strength, for example, can be rapidly brought about by utilising the principle of progressive resistance in weight training. The efficiency of the cardio-vascular and respiratory systems are greatly enhanced by such practices as cross-country running and games playing. In the gymnasium both endurance and strength can be built up effectively by different forms of circuit training and with younger boys similar results can be achieved by the use of obstacle courses. Free-standing work and movement education also have a value in that they exercise and keep supple those smaller muscle groups in the body which sometimes get neglected through too much formal and systematic work. Improved muscle tone and blood supply, which come about as a result of taking exercise through such activities as swimming, athletics and dance, help the digestive and excretory systems to carry out their functions efficiently. A balanced and well-constructed physical education programme which provides exercise in various forms and with varying intensity can go a long way in producing a good state of organic fitness. However it should be remembered that the beneficial effects of exercise such as those we have discussed are not permanent. They are acquired over a period of time and they will disappear over a period of time. It is, therefore, necessary to take exercise regularly if organic fitness is to be maintained. Regrettably this is not the case with many individuals both in and out of school. In the upper sections of some schools, in fact, such are the exigencies of examined subjects for representation on the timetable that little room is left, if any at all, for supervised exercise. Such a state of affairs is to be deplored as inadequate exercise leads not only to a reduction in the efficiency of the organism, but has deleterious effects on the health of the personality.

PHYSICAL GROWTH AND PHYSICAL EDUCATION

Growth, Maturation and Learning

The physical educationist is concerned with all aspects of personality and it is therefore necessary that he understands the meaning and the processes involved in the word growth, for only by doing so will he come to see the intimate nature of the strands that link the educational process with the process of maturation. Intelligent and effective teaching must be closely aware of growth and all that the concept implies.

In order that we may be quite certain what we are talking about, let us begin with a definition. 'Growth is a unifying concept which resolves the dualism of heredity and environment. Environmental factors support, inflect and modify, but they do not generate the progression of development. Growth is an impulsion and as a cycle of morphogenetic events is uniquely a character of the living organism' [36]. Growth is not simply learning or acculturation; nor is it just maturation. It is a product of both working together. Remembering the meaning of the word growth as used by Dewey, the phrase 'working together' is important for it suggests an on-going process and it is in this spirit that the physical educationist should approach his work.

The relative importance of maturation and environment (training, learning, activity, etc.) on growth and behaviour has been the subject of numerous studies. We shall discuss two of them. Each not only clarifies the differences in terms but also has important implications for the physical educationist. The first concerns an experiment by Dennis [37] on the effects of restricted movement on the development of behaviour in infants. The synopsis is given by Hilgard [38]:

A pair of fraternal twins were kept in their cribs from the age of one month until the age of nine months. They were given no training of any kind and only a minimum of handling. They spent most of the time lying on their backs, their hands and feet under the bedclothes. Despite this marked restriction of activity, they developed normally in such behaviour as putting their hands to their mouths, grasping objects, playing with their hands, and sitting up when propped. They were, however, slightly retarded as compared with norms for other children, in the age at which they were able to walk holding on to furniture and in the age at which they were able to stand alone.

The above experiment clarifies the meaning of maturation and underlines its importance as a factor in growth. It should be noted that the infants' reaching was acquired as a result of self-initiated activity. No training or encouragement was given. Dennis concludes that 'the infants' responses are in the main autogenous', meaning that they develop them partially from within themselves and partially through their own activities. It is important for the physical educationist to realise that forms of behaviour and ability arise in this way and more important still, especially in the childhood and adolescent stages of growth, to realise that they can be worked upon and modified as they arise in order that skills may be learnt and adjustments take place.

The experiment just discussed placed the emphasis on restriction of movement. The following experiment concerns a deliberate attempt to study the effects of activity stimulation. For her investigation, which continued for six years, McGraw [39] used the twins, Johnny and Jimmy. Johnny became the experimental subject and was regularly exercised in the early period at two-hourly intervals, whilst the control subject, Jimmy, lay in his crib behind a screen. Later he was left to play with a few toys while Johnny was out swimming, climbing and skating. At certain intervals the relative performance of the two, based on a number of activities, were compared with a view to discovering differences between them. The performances of both were in turn compared to a group of 68 infants who had developed in usual surroundings with an average degree of stimulation. The results may be regarded as coming under two main heads—phylogenetic and ontogenetic.

There was, in general, no significant impact of activity stimulation upon phylogenetic activities, that is to say upon activities which were alike in all infants. Such activities as typical reflexes, grasping with body suspension, crawling, sleeping and walking can be included in this category. The timing of these events and the general pattern of them were similar for Johnny and Jimmy and the large group of other

3. The Principle of Functional Asymmetry. This principle recognises that the infant is equipped and capable of facing the world on a frontal plane of symmetry and could become perfectly ambidextrous. The fact that he does not and that instead he develops unidexterity of hand, or foot, or eye does not represent so much an absolute difference in skill as a predilection for stabilised psychomotor orientations. A preference for the right hand in our culture is not because of an incapability to learn with the left but because of the habits and customs of our culture. It is largely the result of directed functionalism (i.e. education), rather than a natural predilection.

It is a fact that most people are not totally consistent on one side or the other in their acquisition of skills. In my own case, I play squash with my right hand and shoot a bow and arrow with my left. This latter case arose presumably because I was not specifically directed. The implication for the parent/teacher is that since our culture has a predisposition to the right-handed operator it is in the main, on grounds of convenience, best to orientate teaching in that direction. From the biological viewpoint, it is perhaps preferable to cultivate skills on both sides so that muscular harmony can be achieved. It should be stressed too that, neurologically speaking, there is equal facility for developing either side and this, of course, can be done and is done where injury has caused damage to the orientated side.

4. The Principle of Individuating Maturation. This principle reminds us of the mechanism by which the child achieves its particular individuality. As with Lewin's biosphere [44], the child becomes progressively differentiated from his fellows with every new maturational change and accompanying environmental experience. Increasingly specialised functions emerge for him out of a general, but unique, background of experience. The fact that environmental factors, as Gesell makes clear, 'support, inflect and specify' but do not alter the basic maturation sequence makes the environment an important factor in the education of children. The parent/teacher should therefore attempt to create a rich, stimulating and emotionally secure environment in which the child may develop in a healthy as well as in a distinct way.

5. The Principle of Self-Regulatory Fluctuation. This principle gives expression to the fact that the maturing organism does not advance in a straight line or along an even course. It is

often in a state of formative instability which results in fluctuating progressions towards maturity. Although these fluctuations sometimes appear to retreat from a locus of maturity which the child had already attained, such apparent retrogressions should be looked at against a broad frame of time. Since fluctuation is a normal phenomenon the parent/teacher need not get alarmed. Nor must he or she try to infer or communicate fears to the child about its progress. Any such manifestations of concern, particularly in the case of the mother, can, according to Ribble [45], form the basis of emotional maladjustment.

Growth, Norms and Developmental Age

After researching for many years on growth in children, Gesell and his colleagues were led to construct a table of developmental 'norms' which could be regarded as a reference by which a child's developmental record could be checked. In their two complementary volumes [46], the physical educationist can check to see what is normal at the age of 10. This, it must be stressed, is only a guide and should not be interpreted too rigidly. As we have seen, growth is continuous, interrelated and individual in its passage. Maturity emerges with a certain cohesiveness among its many variables. The physical educationist should, therefore, avoid expectancies or make decisions based upon 'averages'. In education each child should be treated as an individual. The physical educationist should also remember that the level and complexity of activity in a programme should not only depend upon the maturation of the neuromuscular system, but upon the child's social, emotional and intellectual maturity as well.

In an attempt to establish 'developmental norms' as opposed to 'age norms' Wetzel [47] designed a grid upon which a child's growth record could be plotted. If the child's progress is satisfactory, entries keep within the appropriate lane alloted to the child on the basis of its body build. If development progresses unsatisfactorily it is revealed on the grid and an enquiry can be held into the possibility of developmental difficulties in the form of such things as malnutrition, disease or anxiety. In addition, therefore, to being an aid to check on a child's development it can also act as a diagnostic tool. A tool such as this can be of real value to the physical educationist in the

practical business of selecting children of compatible developmental age for games and in sending children who show signs of
abnormal growth to the doctor. It is by no means a perfect
instrument as has been shown by Wear and Miller [48],
because, as they point out, equal developmental age does not
necessarily mean equal physical ability. Even so, as a means of
selection it is fairer than a system based upon chronological age.

Principles of Growth
Emerging from our discussions on growth come certain
principles which the physical educationist would do well to
remember if his teaching is to be based on an understanding of
his pupils' development rather than upon just an appraisal of it.
They may be simply stated as follows:

1. Growth is a continuous process.
2. Growth follows an orderly sequence.
3. Growth is characterised by fluctuations.
4. The rate of growth in individual children differs.
5. Growth occurs in a holistic manner.
6. Growth is accompanied by a change in behaviour patterns.

Exercise and Growth
Growth, as we have seen, is affected both by intrinsic or
maturational factors and by extrinsic or environmental factors.
One of the extreme factors of especial interest to the physical
educationist apart from nutrition, illness and sleep, is exercise.
Earlier we made reference to the beneficial effects of exercise
on muscle and bone growth. Here I wish to look at some other
effects of exercise on growth. Adams [49] has shown that 100
women who had engaged in heavy labour since childhood in
the southern plantations of the U.S.A. were not only taller and
heavier but showed larger muscle girths, chest dimensions,
knee width and hip width than a similar number of women
who had not. Several studies [50], too, have demonstrated that
when one limb is used and the other neglected as in playing
tennis, for example, a difference in bone structure and muscular
development emerges. The importance of these studies to the
physical educationist is twofold. Firstly, too much specialism in
function can lead to disproportionate development. If this
cannot be altogether prevented it can at least be offset by a

balanced or if necessary a compensatory programme of work. Secondly, regular and hard work over a period of time can, it seems, produce permanent structural alterations. It follows, therefore, that if the physical educationist is to assist in the growth of children to make them bigger and stronger he must follow a vigorous programme over a number of years.

GROWTH AND THE DEVELOPMENT OF MOTOR SKILLS

Maturation and Maturational Phases
In the last section growth was explained as a product of both maturation and learning. The intrinsic factors are particularly prominent in bringing about new behaviour patterns. Although these changing patterns of ability are modified by the environment and by formal teaching they remain essentially a manifestation of maturational forces. It is important for the physical educationist to understand this if he is to guide and shape the unfolding nature of motor abilities.

The alteration in functional ability with increasing maturity may be simply demonstrated by making reference to the three main phases of development and taking note of the relative motor abilities that become evident.

INFANCY. Studies by Gesell [51], Bayley [52], Shirley [53] and McGraw [54] agree that the advancement of maturity in the development of motor abilities may be seen in the progressions of movement that lead to an upright posture. Stoddard and Wellman [55], in combining the data from several normative studies, present the following picture. At the age of one month crawling movements are displayed when in the prone position; at two months the infant is able to lift his chest when lying on his stomach; at four months his knees straighten on being held erect; at six months he sits momentarily; at nine months he is able to sit alone and shows signs of creeping; at one year he is able to stand alone for a short time; at fifteen months he can walk alone. By the time he is eighteen months he can climb stairs and at two years can run. Because of the overall agreement in the sequential order of these abilities, it is generally recognised that they spring primarily from maturational forces rather than from social stimulation and learning. At the same time, however, the importance of learning is not overlooked for these motor activities are to some extent dependent upon the child taking notice of his surroundings through his visual, tactual and kinaesthetic senses. The importance of sensory stimulation as an aid to learning is made clearly apparent when it is discovered that blind and blind/deaf children are noticeably behind the 'normal' child in the development of motor abilities. It will be seen then that, although innate mechanisms trigger off the next sequential phase of motor development, perceptual media, acting as an aid, affect its rate and, as we saw earlier, probably its quality as well. It follows, therefore, that even in infancy help in the use of sensory cues can lead to improved performance.

CHILDHOOD. By the age of two or so the child may be expected to have sufficient motor control to bring about some independence of action. Although the rate of growth slows down, the principle of sequential development is maintained. A study by Gutteridge [56] adumbrates the increased range of motor activities that accompany the maturation process. Learning in childhood, it is generally conceded, is of greater significance than in infancy in the development of motor abilities. Essentially though, the characteristic features of motor development in childhood—jumping, hopping, skipping, galloping and throwing—are manifestations of a neuromuscular level of ability to do these things even if the way they are directed is subject to environmental influence. Towards the age of seven a difference in the performance of the sexes reveals itself. Boys tend to do better at jumping and throwing and girls at hopping, skipping and galloping.

ADOLESCENCE. It is generally true to say that after the age of five or thereabouts no new activities emerge even though the quality of them may improve and the use to which they are put vary. Although the nature of the activities does not alter, the level of performance does. With an increase in size so the performance improves. When pubescence arrives, however, special features of growth have to be taken into consideration. They have such important consequences for the physical educationist in his efforts to contribute to the growth of the personality that to ignore them would be damaging to his mission. Reference will be made to the other aspects of growth at adolescence in later sections. Here we shall look upon it from the point of view of physiology and motor performance.

Physiological changes at adolescence are numerous and complicated and owing to the paucity of longitudinal data are still imperfectly understood even by the biologists. Whilst the internal chemical changes are beyond the scope of this section, some of the more obvious physical symptoms are not.

It is of practical importance, for example, that the physical educationist should know that just prior to the onset of puberty there is an increased rate of growth in height and weight and at this time there are changes in the body proportions. There is, for instance, a rapid growth of the arms and the legs at first and later this is followed by a surge forward in the growth of the trunk of the body. By the time a boy is thirteen or fourteen years of age his hands and feet have reached almost adult proportions.

At puberty too, the overall shape of the body begins to conform to the appropriate mature contour. The hip width of girls both relatively and absolutely becomes more pronounced and in boys shoulder width gradually comes to predominate over hip width. These changes in shape and size are important in understanding the development of motor performances at adolescence as we shall see later. In addition to these external anthropometrical changes there are psychological ones associated with them and of these we shall also be speaking later. Before we do so, however, let us first return to the problem of how guidance in the early years may best be given.

Guidance of Early Motor Control
We have already noted that motor development is closely related to maturational level. As maturation advances, the opportunity for effective guidance becomes greater and in consequence the role of the parent/teacher becomes more important.

If the infant has been brought up in a good home, the child should have been given the permissive atmosphere to discover his potentialities in the way we indicated earlier. He will have been praised, helped and generally encouraged. The emotional satisfaction he gets from maturational achievements puts him in a conducive frame of mind to improve the quality of the performance which comes with repeated practice. Practice, though, is only significant and helpful to the child if there is an appropriate relationship between the maturational level and the practice or task the parent/teacher sets. Hilgard [57], in attempting to show the connection between maturation and training, after reviewing a number of experimental findings, formulated a series of principles. Some are particularly relevant to our present discussion on the development of motor control. The first three are complementary and are for the most part self-explanatory. They may be stated thus:

1. Skills that build upon developing patterns of behaviour are most easily learned.
2. Training given before maturational readiness may bring about either no improvement or only temporary improvement.
3. Premature training, if frustrating, may do more harm than good.
4. The more mature the organism, the less training is needed to reach a given level of proficiency.

In making further comment about this last principle there are many experiments which suggest that by and large older and more mature children learn faster than younger and less mature children, when given the same amount of practice. This generalisation, it should be made clear, only applies during the period of growth. After adulthood has been reached the reverse may well be true.

At all events the physical education teacher would do well to remember and apply these principles when confronted with a class of different ages and different levels of maturity. In order to make his teaching appropriate he must have a knowledge of the sequential phases of growth and be perceptive enough to realise that, within wide ranges of stimulation (training and encouragement), it is the rate of growth (or maturational level) that determines whether or not a skill can be successfully taught or modified.

So much for the relationship of training or teaching to maturation. Let us now turn our attention to the problem of how best to help the child in bringing on and extending the number of his motor skills both in the home and at school.

Activity is a healthy characteristic of all young children and this manifests itself in their play and in the use of their play materials. So important, in fact, did Jones [58] discover the use of play materials to be in the development of motor skills that she said of them that they 'appear to be the most important extrinsic factor'. Furthermore, in the home itself, she reported that certain conditions seemed to foster the greater use of materials in play activities. These included (a) a playmate from one to three years older than the subject, (b) availability of play materials (this presumably means ready accessibility) and (c) outdoor play space which gives opportunity for freedom of locomotor activities.

It is clear that the child's experience of play materials help considerably in the development of his motor capacities. Because of this the parent/teacher should give some thought to what materials are most suitable to the child's needs and pleasures, bearing in mind his level of maturation. Isaacs [59], after a lifetime in the study of children, makes the following suggestions: old boxes with a movable board for running and jumping off or sliding down; a low railing for climbing and balancing on; balls to kick. Over and above these there might be added such things as swings for swinging, mats for romping and rolling, and quoits for throwing and catching. The main point here is not to make a huge list of possible materials that can be shown to assist with the development of motor skills, but to indicate that some care with the selection of materials should be taken if they are to be of maximum help and value in furthering not only the child's maturational motor capacities but his all-round physical development as well.

Many of the materials so far mentioned should be common to home and school. In both spheres every encouragement should be given to the cultivation and application of such basic motor skills as walking, running, jumping, pulling and pushing, lifting and carrying, throwing and catching, hitting, climbing, swinging and rolling. Munrow [60] has classified skills under six main headings—personal, rhythm, gravity, friction, small object and heavy object. Within this classification fall most of the thirteen movements listed above. It is not our purpose here to examine the nature and categorisation of motor skills, however, but rather to point out that whatever the method is by which the parent/teacher works, suitable provision of materials should be made and adequate time for their use given.

It is perhaps fortunate that the natural inclination of the child is to be active and to indulge of his own accord in many of the activities which we have just mentioned. The first job of the parent/teacher is to provide, as we have seen, a stimulating environment in the form of time, encouragement and materials. If this is done, the child will learn a great deal by his own personal experience especially if he plays in the company of others. In the school situation this process of learning by doing should continue. Instead of the child learning at random, however, the teacher can give balance and direction to the natural impulse of the child and assist him, in an unobtrusive way, not only to improve the quality of his activities but to think about them imaginatively as well as to lead him through interest to higher levels of accomplishment. The Ministry of Education publication *Moving and Growing* [61] gives an excellent insight into many of the activities in which children delight and these can profitably be used by the teacher as a point from which to start his own work. In planning his programme, however, in so far as the development of motor skills is concerned, the physical educationist should not forget that skills tend to be specific and this means that they have to be specifically learnt. As Randall and Waine [62] point out: 'If a skill is worthwhile, then it is better directly approached'. The basic movement approach to physical education has many valuable features about it but, in the realm of specific motor skill learning, has little to offer unless very closely related to the movement in hand.* Even then, as Munrow [63] makes clear, the mere simulation of a skill, e.g. pretending to kick a soccer ball, is not to be equated with the real thing. They are quite different in terms of muscular effort and sensation. This means that even in· kinaesthetic terms the simulated movement is not the same as the real one. All this points to the fact that in the Junior Schools particularly,

* An interesting comment is made by H. Corlett in connection with this point. She says, 'There is no proof that modern educational gymnastics helps in the learning of a specific new skill. What probably is transferable is the attitude of mind, the approach to learning, a better prepared body and the ability to judge what sort of movement is required in a new situation.' (From 'Modern Educational Gymnastics', *Bulletin of Physical Education*, Vol. 5, No. 1, 1960, pp. 11–13.)

the physical educationist should make a deliberate and constructive attempt to teach the motor skills which will be of importance to the child in the years that follow and not spend these critical years only in encouraging the 7–11-year-old to explore his possibilities and to express himself. Opportunities for movement discovery and creativeness should proceed hand in hand with specific or functional skill learning. Bearing in mind the child's maturational level, what materials and implements are suitable for him, and, having some knowledge about the specificity of skill learning, the teacher should proceed without hesitation in the teaching of such skills as will find relevant application in such circumscribed spheres of activity as the games-field, the gymnasium and the swimming bath. If, for example, a skill like passing a rugby ball with accuracy can be mastered in the Junior School, the child will leave with an appreciable accomplishment in hand and a confidence that will serve him in good stead in the Secondary School years ahead.

Motor Ability as a function of Age and Sex

So far we have confined our discussion to the development of motor skills as a product of maturation and environment. In this section we shall come to see that there are other factors involved which the physical educationist, especially at the secondary school level, cannot disregard if he is to teach his pupils in an enlightened and understanding manner.

As we have seen, the acquisition of motor skills is of singular importance in childhood for to a large extent they reflect the normality of his growth. In adolescence they have been shown [64] to relate strongly to personal and social adjustments. We shall be looking into this aspect of motor proficiency later. It is our particular task here to show that the factors of age and sex have an effect upon the development of motor skills. A number of functional qualities are associated with these two factors and we shall look at each of them in turn.

STRENGTH. It is true that age is to some extent indicative of maturational capacities but equally, with increasing age, there is a relative decrease in the importance of new maturational factors. With the onset of pubescence there is an increase in strength both for boys and girls but, since girls tend to mature some two years or so in advance of boys, their strength at the same age, in the early teens especially, may be quite different. Whereas the strength spurt in girls, according to Jones [65], tends to end with the coming of the menarche, for boys it continues through to the age of 18 or so. Meredith [66] has estimated that between the years 6–18 the strength of girls improves by 260% and for boys 359%. This means that the difference between the sexes is mainly accounted for in the continued increase of the boys' strength during the latter part of the adolescent period. This finding seems to be in keeping with the other findings of Jones that the strength performance of girls rarely improves after the age of 14 or 15. As Tanner [67] observes, though, this may be partially due to a lack of motivation in girls of this age to produce their best performances. In a study by Espenchade [68] it is made quite clear that measures of strength are substantially related to gross motor performances. This is noticeably so in boys where she found a correlation of 0·50 between strength and certain measures of motor skill. She comments that 'undoubtedly strength is an element in gross motor performance but its relative importance is more clearly represented when the influence of common growth factors is eliminated. Differences in the size of correlations for boys and girls are probably due in part at least to the relative levels of maturity in the sexes.'

We shall discuss implications for the physical educationist in the matter of strength and in other qualities at the end of this chapter.

REACTION TIME. Studies by Goodenough [69] and Philip [70] reveal the general picture that reaction time in both sexes improves with age and that boys tend to be from 3 to 5% better than girls. Reaction time may partially be understood in maturational terms and partially in learning terms. From a study by Wild [71] on throwing, for example, it would be logical to suppose that the economic movements of the skilled performer could be done in less time than the clumsy movements of the unskilled performer.

CO-ORDINATION. It is obvious that co-ordination is related to the development of motor skills. The control, timing, and rhythm required to execute a tennis smash or a pole vault are plain to see. Although co-ordination is a quality that can be observed and appreciated, however, it is not easily measured. Some aspects of this quality can be examined with the aid of the Brace test [72] of general motor ability.* The twenty movements comprising the test claim to measure the ability of the individual to handle his own body. Findings from the use of the tests show an increasing ability as children get older, the girls keeping pretty well with the boys except in movements of agility involving rapid changes of direction in which the boys are markedly superior. Prepubescent boys in a study by Dimock [73] whose ages were in the main 12 and 13, actually scored higher than boys older and more physiologically advanced. As Espenchade [74] says, 'Explanations of this temporary retardation of growth in motor control may be looked for in rapidly changing body proportions, unequal growth of limb and muscles, inadequate synthesis of changing kinaesthetic perceptions, or changes in the body image'.

BALANCE. As every parent knows, balance plays a conspicuous part in the gradual assumption of the upright walking posture in the infant. It may be thought of as a co-ordinated neuromuscular response which is closely associated with the visual, tactual and kinaesthetic senses. The difference in the ability of children to balance statically or dynamically varies considerably. Evidence by Heath [75] suggests that this quality too increases in the age range of 6–14 with boys improving more than girls. As with co-ordination there is some reason to suppose that at puberty boys may be temporarily retarded.

FLEXIBILITY. It is difficult to know whether flexibility as measured in the various body areas is due to maturation or to the stretching that children undergo in play or in their directed physical activities. A study by Hupprich [76] on girls from the age of 6–18 showed that with a number of exceptions the age at which flexibility is most marked is 12. At this age the

* Recent research casts doubt upon the concept of 'general motor ability'. For a detailed examination of this subject see the article by E. A. Fleishman and W. E. Hempel called 'A Factor Analysis of Physical Proficiency and Manipulative Skill', in *The Journal of Applied Psychology*, Vol. 39, No. 1, 1955, pp. 12–16.

greatest flexibility was shown to be in the areas of the hip, lower back, side, trunk, head, elbow, wrist, ankle and leg abduction.

ORGANIC FITNESS. In a study by Jokl and Cluver [77] on the age range of 5–20 in both sexes they found that in the case of endurance, measured by a 600-yard run, both boys and girls improved to the age of 13. From this age onwards boys continued to improve whereas the girls got progressively worse so that in the period from 17–20 they were no better than 6 to 8-year-olds. This decline in efficiency was not only reflected in their running time but in their physical condition as revealed by their pulse rate, respiration and fatigue. It seems likely that this decline in motor ability stems more from their habits and practices on entering adolescence than from any biological change. Physical prowess and muscular activities for adolescent girls are, it seems, very much subordinated to their social activities and their aspirations towards womanhood. It is not perhaps surprising, therefore, that their organic fitness should deteriorate at this stage in their development.

FUNDAMENTAL MOTOR SKILLS. Activities like sprinting, jumping and throwing are common elements in many forms of games. Furthermore, throughout the period of growth the normal child has opportunities for the development of these capacities. Thus they may be taken as some indication of motor ability, though of course it must be recognised that training, interests and attitudes play an important part in whatever performance is achieved in individual cases. Allowing for these considerations, however, Espenchade [78] has summated a number of studies in these basic fields of activity and presents the following picture. From the age of 6 upwards to 18, boys continue to improve whilst girls show improvement only until about the 13th year when their speed at running is at a maximum. In the other activities they either remain pretty well on a plateau with the increase in age or gradually deteriorate. As with endurance, it seems more likely that a dropping off in performance in the case of girls is due more to cultural influences than to structural alteration or the development of secondary sex characteristics.

Educational Implications

At the end of the opening section of this book we spoke of the need for the respect of human personality. One of the inviolable rights of the personality is that it should be free to grow. In this section we have followed through in some detail the physical aspect of growth and have noted that with growth there accrue changes in thought as well as in performance. While we have confined our attention in the main to general trends, it is clear too that there are very big individual differences. The physical educationist should be fully aware of both matters and plan his teaching accordingly.

We have noticed that in pretty well all of the elements that are related to development in motor skills, improvement takes place with an increase in age. This applies to both sexes until the age of 13 or so. The physical educationist can accordingly expect a graph of progression until this age no matter what the quality of his teaching is like, for improvement up until this age is primarily a question of maturation. However, with his encouragement, technical knowledge, and teaching ability, he can frequently bring about improvements on raw maturational capacities. He is often able to do this by turning to good account knowledge of growth such as that we have just discussed. For example, we discovered that, contrary to expectation, the age at which girls showed the greatest amount of flexibility was 12. This being the case he would be wise to start those skills that require a high degree of flexibility before or at this time if the full potential in this sphere of activity is to be reached. Similarly, remembering that the reaction time of boys is slightly better than that for girls, it would be theoretically unfair to oppose them in competition. In practice, however, as the Espenschade fundamental motor skills chart [78] shows, there is little sex differentiation, except in the distance throw, until secondary school age is reached. Joint participation can, therefore, be carried on quite profitably as indeed it is in many Primary Schools. With the coming of adolescence the continued improvement of the boys in all qualities, apart from possibly balance and co-ordination, and the relative stagnation of the girls, makes joint participation, except at a social level, quite impossible. Even within the sexes there are extremely large individual differences in motor ability and these differences may be greater, comparatively speaking, than the differences in intelligence. With the passing of time and the influence of technical accomplishment and motivation being added to maturational ability, the differences can become so marked that 'setting' not only in classes but between forms may become desirable.*

The woman teacher of physical education will perhaps be less distressed and despondent when she observes the falling off in performance and interest as the adolescent girl gets older, if she understands that this is a normal concomitant to this phase of the growth process. The man teacher of physical education may also experience in the middle and late adolescent boy a lack of interest in many of the more usual round of activities but, in keeping with the culture's esteem for physical prowess, he will work hard to be strong and to shine at those activities which carry status in the community of which he is a member.

No matter whether the physical educator is a teacher of both boys and girls or only boys or only girls, certain tenets of good teaching should characterise his work in this field as in others. He should aim to:

1. Choose activities in keeping with the child's maturational level.

2. Capitalise on interests already present and take notice of those that come about as a result of biological change.

3. Set purposeful and progressive targets upon which the child can set his sights and with hard work be sure of success.

4. Allow the child to explore and to discover things for himself although in the realm of technical skills it is best that teaching should be specific.

5. Give praise and encouragement when it is deserved so that the child is given a feeling of recognition. (The satisfaction of this puts him in the right frame of mind to continue learning.) Conversely, criticism should be kept to a minimum and observations should always be constructive.

* There are points for and against physical education classes being arranged in ability groups. These are clearly set down in *Issues in Physical Education* by M. A. Sanborn and B. G. Hartman, Lea and Febinger, 1964, pp. 164–7.

6. Remember that the development of motor skills is an important area in the child's personality development and that other areas, emotional and social for example, are related to it.

SOMATOTYPES AND INDIVIDUAL DIFFERENCES

Physique and Temperament

One aspect of the development of motor abilities deliberately left out of our discussions in their relationship to growth is the question of body build. Problems of individual differences impinge themselves considerably upon the minds of educators. In physical education the somatotype a pupil has is of fundamental importance. Every teacher knows that what can be reasonably expected from one pupil cannot, by any stretch of the imagination, be expected from another. The fat, ponderous boy, for example, can in no way compete with the lean agile boy in activities that put a premium on mobility. The teacher must always carry before him the concept of the individual and remember that what is suitable and satisfying for some children is possibly quite unsuitable and hateful for others. Whilst recognising that it is a practical impossibility to please all children all the time, it must nevertheless remain an aim of the teacher to present material that will be of interest and value to all pupils under his care.

From the time of Hippocrates there have been numerous attempts to classify people according to their body build. More recently there have been efforts to show a relationship between body type and personality characteristics. Apart from Kretschmer [79], it would be fair to say that the most outstanding name in this field is that of Sheldon. We shall look at his system of somatotyping first.

Sheldon [80] has presented a method whereby body types may be classified on the basis of the components of endomorphy, mesomorphy and ectomorphy. In this method he makes allowance for the varying amounts of each component which is represented within any individual. This is accomplished by the use of a 7-point scale. Thus a person with a somatotype of 444 would have each component equally represented. A predominantly endomorphic individual would appear fat, round and soft and give the impression of being under moderate pneumatic pressure. He is not well muscled and therefore finds difficulty in those activities that require him to move quickly or overcome his own body weight. His large surface area and low density enables him to float well. Among the temperamental traits, called collectively viscerotonia that Sheldon found to accompany the extreme endomorph are the love of relaxation, comfort, sociability and food.

The characteristics of the typical mesomorph are quite different. His physique is square, rugged and marked by a predominance of muscle and connective tissue. The shoulders are broad and the waist relatively thin. He is strong and physically able. Somatotonia, the temperamental correlate, is marked by a liking for physical adventure, exercise, combat and a tendency towards aggressiveness, directness, assertiveness and action.

The distinct ectomorph can be recognised by his linearity, fragility and delicacy of body composition. His bones are thin and his muscles small. The shoulders are relatively narrow and lack muscle support and padding. Individuals who fall into this category are often agile and have good body control but have not very much resilience in combative forms of activity. The associated temperamental characteristics, generically called cerebrotonia, are marked by a predominance of restraint, inhibition and desire for concealment. Such people are often over reactive, apprehensive and uncertain of themselves in social situations.

Sheldon's physique classifications and their high temperamental correlates (they were all over 0·70) have led a number of psychologists to look upon them somewhat sceptically.

Eysenck [81] has been particularly critical. He points out that there were certain procedural flaws that were inherent in the investigation and that Sheldon's findings have not been proved to be consistent with other peoples'. Even though some aspects of Sheldon's work can be justifiably criticised it is generally conceded that his system of physical classification (or modifications of it) is the best that has yet been devised, while on the temperamental side, although the correlations may not be as high as Sheldon indicated, there is enough evidence to show a clear connection between physique and certain personality traits. Hall and Lindsey [82], for example, after examining all the available evidence have this to say: 'We believe that . . . Sheldon is eminently correct in his assertion that there is a highly significant association between physique and personality.' If this may be taken as a fair appraisal of the situation, it is clearly something the physical educationist cannot afford to ignore.

Physique and Motor Performance

A number of studies [83] designed to ascertain the relationship between somatotype and physical performances have revealed the following to be true. First, the person who has a predominance of endomorphy has a lot of weight to carry and this has been proven to be a severe handicap when indulging in physical activity. Second, the ectomorphic individual is, relatively speaking, muscularly weak, ill-protected, and therefore prone to injury. This makes the number of competitive sports in which he may participate without undue risk necessarily limited. Third, the mesomorphic person is so built that his ruggedness and strength are conducive to outstanding physical performances. In addition to these findings two other points should be mentioned here. One is that what has so far been said is true for women as well as for men. The only difference between the sexes is that women tend more to endomorphy than men. The other is that in Sheldon's system height is a factor that is ignored as his system is primarily based on shape. Where other things are equal the height of the individual is often the feature that differentiates performance, as it does in basketball or shot putting, for instance.

Other factors of Sheldon's somatotyping which may eventually prove to be related to motor performance are gynandromorphy or the degree to which the individual possesses the characteristics of the opposite sex (from observation it is obvious that, structurally speaking, the male kind of female does better than the female kind of female); dyplasia or the extent to which an individual presents different forms of somatotype in the different regions of the body; and aplasia or the degree of arrested or incomplete development. More research is needed in each of these areas.

Where research has been done on outstanding performers

certain types of somatotype have been found to relate to certain events. Cureton [84], for example, in studying champion athletes found that typical track men are slight in skeletal framework with a relatively longer upper leg ratio and a longer leg to trunk relationship than their fellows. He also found that most good sprinters have narrower hips. Men who were weight-lifters, wrestlers, gymnasts and divers tended to have longer and larger trunks than the others. These general observations were, by and large, substantiated by Tanner [85]. He found that the throwers as a group were taller and heavier and had larger muscles in relation to their limb bones and longer arms in relation to their legs. As he observes after setting out the details of his findings, 'The explanation of the physical differences between highly successful athletes in the different events must evidently lie in the differing mechanical and physiological requirements of the tasks'. In the case of the discus, for example, where speed at the moment of release is so important, the speed is proportional to the length of the 'lever' throwing the implement. Thus the person with broad shoulders and long arms will have an advantage over somebody else not so well endowed. Similarly in other events other forms of structural advantage have their effect. Mechanical advantages of this sort predispose certain types of physique to success in events that are particularly suited to them.

In the majority of studies outstanding performers have been somatotyped at the outset and afterwards been associated with a particular event or sport. In an attempt to start from the other direction and include average and poor performers, Arnold [86] carried out an investigation on pre-adolescent schoolboys. For several years he gave the new intake at his school a battery of tests (strength, speed, balance, muscular power, general ability) in order to give each child a general physical ability rating on a 6-point scale. The second phase of the experiment involved finding the individual and average somatotype for children falling within each of the six physical ability categories. The overall picture emerged that the children with the highest ability rating had also the highest mesomorphic content. In general it was found that as the physical ability grade got lower so the strength of the meso-morphic component diminished. Findings indicated that, if the relative strength of the three components are taken into account, the following pattern presents itself as a guide to general physical capacity.*

The stronger component is placed first:

Meso
Meso/Ecto
Ecto/Meso
Meso/Endo
Endo/Meso
Endo
Endo/Ecto

On the biological side there is some evidence provided by Tanner [87] and others that mesomorphy is associated with early maturity. This may be an additional explanation of why, especially at school, the children high in mesomorphy do so well at physical activities.

As far as teachers of physical education go, both Parnell [88] and Carter [89] have shown that they are drawn mainly from the ranks of people with predominantly mesomorphic build.

Educational Implications
The section concerned with physique and temperament perhaps brought out the point that this was another approach to understanding the puzzle of personality development. Each child must be seen as an individual who lives amongst other individuals, if we are to help him towards optimum progress. It is clear that in physical education a wide choice of activities must be offered if the potential interests of children are to be met. The teacher who directs unwilling pupils into teams to satisfy his own enthusiasm or because he has a misguided notion about honouring the school's name is not doing his duty. Ideally as wide a range of facilities as possible should be available and some choice of activity given. It is good, of course, in the early years, that children should be introduced and exposed to different forms of activity—in a compulsory way if necessary—but in the upper forms of secondary schools, by which time individual differences have become still more pronounced, a

* If, in addition to the five tests, account is taken also of each boy's ability in games, gymnastics, swimming and athletics a slightly truer overall picture is formed.

limited choice should be given. It should be recognised, for example, that the cerebrotonic ectomorph is suited neither structurally nor temperamentally to tough combative sports like rugby and should accordingly be offered a choice of activity in the non-combative range, like basketball or tennis. This is not to say that it should be automatically presumed that ecto-morphs do not want to participate in combative sports. Often they do for various reasons. If this is the case they should be allowed to. But because of the wide range in strength and skill between individuals, the teacher should take care to see that unfair competition does not arise.

As Arnold's investigations, demonstrate the mesomorphic content of a person's somatotype is often a good indication of his physical ability. This being so, the knowledge of the somatotype of an individual can often help in the selection of homogeneous physical groupings for such activities as games. If, at the Secondary School stage, groupings are based upon similarities in somatotype, the teacher can often more easily produce a programme of activities that will meet the needs and abilities of the group—particularly if size is taken into account. By using such a system it becomes theoretically possible to place together people who have an affinity in outlook and functional capacity. Such a form of segregation is practicable but it is doubtful whether selection based upon this criterion alone is educationally sound. Motivational factors, special abilities and other good reasons would always act against a system based upon such an arbitrary division. At best it may be said that a knowledge of personality traits can help a teacher to under-stand his pupils better and help guide them towards activities for which they are most suited. To some very keen but dis-heartened children it may even be necessary, on occasions, to point out to them that their lack of success in a particular activity may be due to a limited structural potentiality, and that they should try some other activity to which they are more anatomically suited.

Physical education teachers can also learn something about themselves from an acquaintance with studies to do with somatotyping. Earlier we made reference to the fact that teachers of physical education tend to be recruited from that section of the population which is predominantly mesomorphic. The educational import of this is well posed by Parnell's question [*90*], 'How are teachers of physical education to acquire a comprehensive outlook if their background in physique and culture deprives them of "inborn" understanding of two-thirds of their pupils with different somatotypes?' Clearly, in view of all that has been said, the question is a justifiable one. The answer to it is that the teacher should make himself aware of the dangers: firstly, by an acquaintance with the literature on the subject, and secondly, by applying that knowledge with imagination. If, in addition, he can keep before him the ethic of the respect for the personality he should not go too far wrong.

BOOKS FOR FURTHER READING

Clarke, E. H., *Application of Measurement to Health and Physical Education*. Prentice-Hall, 1967.

Cratty, B. J., *Movement Behaviour and Motor Learning*. Kimpton, 1964.

Dalzell-Ward, A. J., 'Physical Activity and Health' in *Readings in Physical Education*. P.E. Association, 1966.

Davis, E. C., et al., *Biophysical Values of Muscular Activity*. W. C. Brown, 1965.

Espenchade, A., 'Motor Development' in *Science and Medicine of Exercise and Sports*. Harper, 1960.

Garrison, K. C., *Growth and Development*. Longmans, 1960.

Gesell, A., 'The Ontogenesis of Infant Behaviour' in *Manual of Child Psychology*. John Wiley & Sons, 1954.

Gesell, A. L., *The First Five Years of Life*. N.Y. Harper, 1940.

—— *The Child from Five to Ten*. N.Y. Harper, 1946.

Hilgard, E. R., *Introduction to Psychology*. Methuen, 1962.

Isaacs, S., *The Nursery Years*. Routledge and Kegan Paul, 1932.

Jahoda, M., *Current Concepts of Positive Mental Health*. Basic Books, 1958.

Karpovich, P. V., Physiology of Muscular Activity. W. B. Saunders, 1965.

Mauldon, E. and Layson, J., *Teaching Gymnastics*. MacDonald and Evans, 1965.

Ministry of Education, *Moving and Growing*. H.M.S.O., 1952.

Munrow, D., *Pure and Applied Gymnastics*. Arnold, 1957.

Murray, G. W. and Hunter, T. A. A., *Physical Education and Health*. Heinemann, 1966.

Pallett, G. D., *Modern Educational Gymnastics*. Pergamon, 1965.

Parnell, R. W., *Behaviour and Physique*. Arnold, 1958.
Randall, M. W. and Waine, W. K., *Objectives of the Physical Education Lesson*. Bell, 1955 (Appendix C: An Evaluation of the Wetzel Grid).
Sheldon, W. H., *The Varieties of Temperament*. Harper, 1942.
—— W. H., *The Varieties of Human Physique*. Harper, 1940.
—— *Atlas of Man*. Harper, 1954.
Tanner, J. M., *Growth at Adolescence*. Blackwell, 1962.
—— *The Physique of the Olympic Athlete*. George Allen and Unwin, 1964.
Williams, J. G. P., *Medical Aspects of Sport and Physical Fitness*. Pergamon, 1965.

CHAPTER THREE

THE MENTAL ELEMENT IN PHYSICAL EDUCATION

THE SENSORY BASIS OF INTELLECTUAL BEHAVIOUR

The intelligence of a person is closely associated with his intellectual abilities. As the child grows older so it is normal for his intelligence to grow and his ability to solve intellectual problems to improve. The one may be regarded as the collateral of the other.

The two factors responsible for the amount of intelligence we have at any one time are those of heredity and environment. Numerous attempts have been made to ascertain the relative importance of each but none has been entirely satisfactory. Vernon [91], however, after a review of all the relevant evidence to do with this problem, came to the conclusion that about 25% of intelligence as measured by intelligence tests could in certain cases be ascribable to environmental circumstances. The other 75% in general terms could be attributed chiefly to inborn genetic structuring. The hereditary factor or innate potential Hebb [92] calls intelligence A, and what is actually measured (a product of both heredity and environment) he calls intelligence B. It is clear, if we may take this as an approximation of the position, that it is the environmental side with which education is primarily concerned and, leaving aside such matters as nutrition, rest, warmth and so on, it is the home and school that are especially significant in their influence.

Even in babyhood it is apparent that the physical element in education is of crucial importance, for as Ribble [93] says, 'the appropriate stimulation of the senses leads to getting a sense of the self and of the world of physical objects, as well as to beginning to feel a sense of personal relationships'. In many hospitals today it has become a rule that every baby should be picked up, patted and fondled for it is now recognised that if babies are left for long periods without individual attention and stimulation they can fall into a state of mental atrophy. Research workers at the Pestalozzi Village for refugee children at Trogen [94], for example, found that a period of neglect 'slows down or arrests the development of the emotional life and thus in turn inhibits normal intellectual development'. Further evidence that the sensory or physical aspect of healthy personality development is of importance comes from Bowlby [95]. Although he speaks of maternal deprivation as being injurious to physical, emotional, social and intellectual development of the child, it gradually becomes clear that it is the physical warmth and comfort with friendly sensory stimulation that is required. This, as he acknowledges, can be given as well by a mother substitute as by the true mother. It is only, however, when we examine what it is that a mother (or substitute mother) does, or is expected to do, in bringing up her child that we come to realise how much of it revolves round the 'physical' and is manifested by such practices as picking up, cuddling, fondling and playing. The researches of Bowlby and others show that the absence of such practices in early upbringing can lead to impaired intellectual functioning and disturbed mental health. Such consequences may not only stem from maternal deprivation. Evidence by Andry [96] and Bradley [97] suggests that the father's role in this respect may be more important than has hitherto been admitted.

Complementing those researches to do with child development are those to do with perception. It will be seen that since perception is largely connected with the senses, including the kinaesthetic, it has a good deal in common with the physical aspects of education. The senses, in fact, when taken together, form the apparatus by which we gather information about our environment and form the basis of our learning and understanding. Hebb [98], working mainly with young animals, has shown that if the senses are prevented from being used learning capacity is affected. This sensory deprivation not only affects the accumulation of experience at the time but may well have a significant effect upon 'the overall capacity to achieve mature intelligence' later. If this is so—and it ties up with Bowlby's evidence—it becomes apparent that sensory experience in the early years is of critical importance to intellectual growth. That a favourable sensory environment is desirable for efficient mental functioning for human adults as well as for young animals is clear from an experiment conducted by Bexton, Heron and Scott [99]:

> The subject is paid to do nothing for 24 hours a day. He lies on a comfortable bed in a small closed cubicle, is fed on request, goes to the toilet on request. Otherwise, he does nothing. He wears frosted glasses that admit light but do not allow pattern vision. His ears are covered by a sponge-rubber pillow in which are embedded small speakers by which he can be communicated with, and a microphone hangs near to him to enable him to answer. His hands are covered with gloves and cardboard cuffs extend from the upper forearm beyond his finger tips, permitting free joint movement but with little tactual perception. The results are dramatic. During the stay in the cubicle, the experimental subject shows extensive loss, statistically significant, in solving problems. He complains subjectively that he cannot concentrate; his boredom is such that he looks forward eagerly to the next problem, but when it is presented he finds himself unwilling to solve it.
>
> On emergence from the cubicle the subject is given the same kind of intelligence tests as before entering and shows significant loss. There is a disturbance of motor control. Visual perception is changed in a way difficult to describe; it is as if the object looked at was exceptionally vivid, but impaired in its relationship to other subjects and the background—a disturbance perhaps in the organisation of perception. This condition may last up to 12 or 24 hours.

This evidence and other evidence—notably by Schaffer [100] working with human infants—indicates strongly that an absence of adequate sensory stimuli can have temporary detrimental intellectual effects and maybe permanent ones as well. Hebb [101], indeed, states quite categorically that as far as mammals are concerned 'perceptional restriction in infancy certainly produces a low level of intelligence'. When, in addition, we learn from Guilford [102], that one of the varieties of intelligence measured by psychometric tests is kinaesthetic perception, and from Piaget [103] that sensorimotor activity is a form of practical intelligence, it becomes hard to see how early physical activity can fail to contribute towards the growth of overall intelligence and thus to overall intellectual functioning. Without the aid of experimental data educational pioneers like Pestalozzi, Froebel, Montessori and the McMillan sisters were able to see this for themselves and produce forms of education that took cognizance of it. More recently still, Wall [*104*] has noted that 'the contribution of the home and the nursery school to the child's intellectual development should arise naturally out of the quality of the environment they provide rather than from any direct teaching such as may be given in primary or secondary schools'. Such an environment should be as rich in its sensory stimulation as it is warm in its emotional climate.

Since play, when properly guided, provides conditions similar to those mentioned above, it must be studied carefully as an educational medium to see how it contributes to intellectual development.

PLAY AND THE GROWTH OF UNDERSTANDING IN THE YOUNG CHILD

From the very beginning the self-initiated activity of the infant brings to him sensations and a widening perception of his environment. He kicks; he explores; he discovers himself and other people. More than this he makes his acquaintance with things and objects. As the weeks and months pass he extends his knowledge of the material world. All the time he is assimilating information and learning. The impressions and experiences he derives from his actions form the basis of his thoughts. 'Providing the environment is a suitable one,' says Mellor [*105*], 'it is as natural for mental growth and learning to take place as it is for physical growth, and we need have no more anxiety about the one than the other.' The important question arising from such a statement is to decide what sort of environment is suitable. Our previous discussions indicated that it must involve a secure emotional atmosphere and adequate sensory stimulation. To make such a provision in infancy is not too difficult a problem. The mother by her handling and attention is able to meet what is required on both scores. With the coming of increased mobility in childhood, however, and the insatiable desire for activity, the problem is that much harder. Experience of *any* sort, as we saw earlier, is not enough. It must be profitable and lead to the on-going process of growth. If traumatic and damaging forms of experience are to be avoided, it is clear that some guidance (preferably indirect) must be given. The child must feel himself free to be active and yet be safe in the knowledge that he is secure. Play activity provides the freedom and the unobtrusive parent/teacher the security. Granted these suitable environmental conditions, it seems that play may be looked upon not only as a medium through which education can take place but as a mirror in which one can see reflected the results of learning.

The 'prepared environment' with its water, sand, clay, blocks and open spaces positively enhances sensory and other forms of experiences so that the intelligence and intellect become nourished from the richness of the surroundings. As the child goes about his activities he is consciously and unconsciously assimilating information. As if in anticipation of modern psychologists, Pestalozzi [106] observed long ago that 'life educates. Just as moral education begins in inner experiences, i.e. impressions which touch our feelings, so the education of the intellect results from the experience of objects which act as stimuli upon our senses. Nature brings the whole range of our senses to bear impression on life. All our knowledge of the outside world is the result of sensory experience.' More recently Piaget [107] has shown how the mental development of the child is intimately linked to his maturation and to his interaction with the environment. He sees the child as an agent in his own development. In his play the child can be seen to explore with his hand, eye and mouth. The results of his own activities are accompanied by associated mental patterns. This process of absorbing and organising Piaget calls 'assimilation'. He regards it as a fundamental process of learning and growth. At the same time, however, this process of assimilation is being modified by the child's confrontation with new situations or objects which necessitate a change in the existing patterns of his mind. This process of alteration is called 'accommodation'. Thus, taken together, the two processes of assimilation and accommodation are, for Piaget, the chief controlling factors of intellectual growth and constitute what he terms as 'adaptation'. The rich and stimulating variety of play activity, as Piaget acknowledges, is a basic source of intellectual growth.

Whilst recognising that the nature of intelligence is probably more complex than those aspects of intelligence that intelligence tests claim to measure, it has nevertheless been shown by Thurston [108] that when the items comprising intelligence tests are analysed no less than seven primary abilities can be identified. These are verbal comprehension, word fluency, number, space, memory, perception and reasoning. It is because the very nature of play demands these self-same abilities that play may be said to further if not foster the growth of intelligence and thus make a contribution to the child's intellectual advancement. Leaving aside the complications of Piagetian theory for a moment, let us look at the child as he may be observed. His intellectual energies centre around his curiosity. As he moves about he investigates things and makes discoveries. He learns, for example, that water is wet, that it runs downhill and that it can't be picked up unless it is contained in something. He will perhaps learn too, that when it is very cold, water can turn into ice and can be used for cooling drinks and for sliding upon. The teacher's role in the 'prepared environment', as Montessori called it, is to encourage such discoveries to occur and, if called upon, to help in the explanation of puzzling phenomena. But play is not just learning through experience. It frequently quickens the interest and keeps alive the voracity of the human intelligence. Depending upon the emotio-social accompaniments of learning associations too, attitudes and sentiments towards objects and things can be found that may hinder or enhance his approach to intellectual problems at a later stage. The accommodation of Piaget is not so far removed from the conditioning procedures of Pavlov and Watson. A knowledge of materials then, with their distinctive properties and uses, helps the child to understand the whole world about him. He gives his attention and concentration to things that intrigue him and memorises those things which experience has taught him to have importance. Curiosity, otherwise perhaps in abeyance, often derives from his own motor activities and takes him forward in his learning in quite unexpected ways. As Dewey [109] says: 'Thinking begins as soon as the baby who has lost the ball he is playing with begins to foresee the possibility of something not yet existing—its recovery, and begins to forecast steps towards the realisation of this possibility, and, by experimentation, to guide his acts by his ideas and thereby also test his ideas'. Thus, it may be added, the result of a physical act can sometimes initiate an elementary process of reasoning. The one can often be a consequence of the other. Play in general, and physical education in particular, abound with situations where action or the inability to act efficiently require thought and reason.

Language used in its widest sense is self expression and communication. Play, it has been said, is the natural form of expression of the child. He stamps in anger and jumps with joy. Such forms of bodily expression often externalise his emotional state. They may also be a means whereby the child gets to comprehend words. He may, for example, through repetition, come to associate going out of doors with the word 'outside' and the coming back in again with the word 'inside'. Memory and verbal comprehension alike proceed by the use of such word pairings as 'up' and 'down', 'fast' and 'slow' which arise out of play activities. The symbolic use of language, it is generally conceded, is not only a measure of the child's intellectual level but is also an aid to his thinking. Watson [110] even went so far as to claim, at one time, that thinking is merely sub-vocal talking. Later he modified this extreme view by saying that 'thinking at successive moments of time may be kinaesthetic, verbal or emotional'. Either way, it seems that activity, whether it provokes new words or whether it assists thought through the use of kinaesthetic imagery, is an aid to intellectual functioning. Be this as it may, the background from which good verbal development comes is associated with the richness of the environment.* The variety of materials, the amount of conversation with other children, the emotional climate of the home all have an effect on verbal fluency and comprehension. A still greater factor is probably the degree and quality of contact children have with adults. McCarthy [111] has shown, for example, that the children of lower socio-economic groups are linguistically less gifted than those from the higher socio-economic groups. Leaving aside the possible difference in innate intelligence McCarthy puts this down to the two factors:

* For an account of how an impoverished environment can effect language see Bernstein, B. B., 'Social Class and Linguistic Development' in Halsey, A. H., Floud, J. and Anderson, C., Education, Economy and Society Free Press, N.Y., 1961.

that the parents of the less gifted groups are firstly, less linguistically gifted themselves and therefore provide a poor model
and secondly, that they provide less stimulation. All this
points to the fact that play activities should, especially in
middle and later childhood, be well directed emotionally,
materially and verbally, if the activities themselves are
in turn to lead to further intellectual advancement. As
Piaget says, a reciprocity exists between the child's assimilation and accommodation and between his doing and his
learning.

Another symbolic process is that of number. In his games and
play activities the child will often come across such words as
'two', 'five', 'big', 'small', 'heavy', 'light' and phrases like 'a
few', 'too many', and 'half a dozen'. Gradually they come to
have significance for him and later he will be taught to associate
the appropriate symbol with the comprehended word. To give
the child real understanding of what numbers mean he has to
handle and experience them so that they can become personalised, noticed and remembered. In a skipping or catching game,
for example, the number of successful repetitions can provoke
the desire to count and to record. The teacher should always be
at hand to assist him in these endeavours. The urge to construct
often necessitates a better appreciation of space, distance and
number. In a self-imposed task such as making a sand castle the
child is called upon to learn how to measure, to appreciate space
and to exercise his imagination and inventive powers. Play with
its manifold activities constantly calls upon old learning and
stimulates new learning. Mental consolidation and growth go
on hand in hand.

Make believe play gives the child a greater understanding of
the world about him. By projecting himself into the role of a
coalman, a bricklayer or shopkeeper he gains an insight into the
life and function of other people. He observes and he imitates
and imitation, as Miller and Dollard [112] have shown, is
closely related to learning.

In all the games and play activities in which the child
indulges, the child's restlessness for knowledge will lead him to
ask questions. If the parent/teacher's answers are given skilfully
and aptly, a good deal of information can be suitably conveyed
into the mind of the child so that he can use it as a springboard
for additional intellectual progress.

Play, through its physical activity, enables the senses to assist with the learning process and, by the stimulating and problem provoking situations it arouses, provides a positive contribution not only to the mental powers and intellectual processes, but to the integration of the child's personality by engaging it in a psychosomatic unity.

MOTOR LEARNING IN PHYSICAL EDUCATION

Basic considerations of Motor Learning
In the last chapter we noted that such factors as age, sex and somatotype all play a part in the development of motor skills. But there are a number of other factors which are more concerned with the learning side of skill acquisition.

INTELLIGENCE. It is often assumed by teachers that the more intelligent child is able to pick things up more readily than the less intelligent child. Although this may be true in most learning situations evidence seems to suggest that in the realm of sensori-motor skills there is less justification for this assumption. Indeed, Munn [*113*] after examining a number of experiments concludes: 'Investigations of the relation between intelligence test performance and learning of sensori-motor skills in young children agree in forcing the conclusion that at early states at least, there is no significant correlation'. This comment, it should be emphasised, applies chiefly to those years when maturational effects of skill development are at their most powerful and therefore may give a slightly distorted impression. That this viewpoint is to some extent justified is apparent when we look at experiments conducted on children of pre-adolescent ages. Kulcinski [*114*], for example, has reported 'a definite and positive relationship' between various degrees of intelligence of 11- and 12-year-old boys and girls and the learning of fundamental muscular skills of the tumbling and stunt variety. Regrettably he does not give further details. In the investigation conducted by Arnold [*115*], to which reference has been made earlier, no positive connections were established between the physical ability test scores and intelligence test scores although it is perhaps not without significance to record that all the boys who were in the top two of the six physical ability grades were above the group's average in intelligence. Working with educationally sub-normal boys aged between 12–15, Oliver [*116*] found positive correlations between intelligence as measured by the Terman and Porteus tests and an athletic achievement test which comprised a 50-yard dash, a standing broad jump and throwing the cricket ball. The correlations were 0·15 and 0·32 respectively after the age factor had been extracted. In another test—the tennis test—in which the exercise of intelligence, it seems, could be demonstrated more clearly, further correlations were shown. These were 0·07 with the Terman test and 0·40 with the Porteus Maze test. In looking at these results we must remember that they were obtained from a sample of backward children and that for normal children the relationship between intelligence and physical skills may not be so obvious. Even so it is not unreasonable to suggest that some degree of intelligence must exist in the learning of motor skills otherwise no *learning* would take place at all. Any skills that developed would simply be products of maturation. A more tenable position might well be this. For 'normal' children there appears to be no great premium upon intelligence in the learning of motor skills but as the amount of intelligence in any one individual or group of people diminishes it seems possible, bearing in mind Oliver's findings, that its relative importance becomes greater. This, however, is speculation. It is clear that a good deal more research needs to be done in this field.

In making some general observations it appears that there is little evidence to support the belief that intelligence is very much connected to the acquisition of physical skills in normal children, especially in the early years, although it may be more noticeably related in and towards the period of adolescence. Where instructions are given it is credible to suppose that intelligence must play its part in comprehending them. Also, as Knapp [*117*] says after an appraisal of this topic, 'as skills become more complex and require more organisation and understanding and particularly when decision making becomes important, the relationship tends to increase . . .' But even then, as she points out, it is rarely substantial.*

MOTIVATION. Motivation is an important factor in any learning situation and not least of all in physical education. It comprises a vast and complex field of research and we can do no more than touch upon it here. There are, however, some practical aspects of it that can be profitably discussed.

In the first place it should be made clear that the educationist is not only concerned with results. He is also concerned with values. It is, therefore, important to him that skill learning should take place in the 'right' way as well as in an effective way. In doing this he must ideally attempt to teach skills by pointing out their intrinsic worth. He must try to convey the thought that throwing the javelin, in the best possible manner, for example, is worth while for its own sake. Encouraging children to take up activities for the extrinsic reasons of administration, school representation or gaining a school colour and so on, may prove to be effective but, educationally speaking, it is doubtful if the means can be said to justify the ends. Education after all is concerned with attitudes and values as well as with performance. It is something of a relief to find, when temptations are so strong in this direction, that the psychologists agree that throughout childhood there is an impulsive urge to be active and that this to some extent makes redundant the artificial devices of the teacher to gain interest. It seems, too, according to Burnett and Pear [118], that there is not only a need to be active but that this activity gives pleasure through the exercise of the proprioceptive and cutaneous organs. The satisfaction thus gained provides an

* Earlier in the century Reaney researched into the possible relationship between general intelligence and play ability in organised group games (hockey and netball for girls; football, hockey and cricket for boys). She had as her subjects 600 children ranging in age from 8 to 18 who were from different schools and social backgrounds. At the end of her study she made the unequivocal statement that 'a definite correlation exists between General Ability and Play Ability for group games'. The correlation she put forward of 0·32 must, however, be viewed with some reservation as 'Play Ability' was assessed by the teachers concerned only on a subjective basis.

Reaney, M. J., 'The correlation between general intelligence and Play Ability as shown in Organised Group Games', B.J.P., Vol. 7, 1914–15, pp. 226–52.

incentive for more activity. This kinaesthetic sensation they call 'muscular sensuousness' and may be regarded by us as a form of intrinsic motivation. When the desire for self expression leads to a skill being learned, as it might easily do in dance for example, then it too can be said to originate intrinsically. Regrettably for the physical educationist not all his work can be inspired by intrinsic springs to be active and it becomes necessary for him to manufacture interest. Such things as giving praise and providing goals which lead to success, if used with discretion, are quite legitimate but such devices as the use of standards, badges and honours can lead to skills being learnt for the sake of the award rather than for the intrinsic value of the activity. Extrinsic forms of motivation should, therefore, be used warily for, though they may bring about improved performances, they may be accompanied by questionable attitudes.

Jacks [119] has remarked 'man is a skill hungry animal' and, in childhood, these skills should be allowed to develop amid joy and laughter so that the technical aspects of later skill acquisition are to be built on a sound psychological base. A skill, once acquired, becomes a part of the person and on this account is not easy to give up. It was perhaps this realisation that led Munrow [120] to say that 'through skill, there is likely to be a more permanent satisfaction and interest in physical acitivity'.

PRACTICE. Numerous experiments [121] in the field of both intelligence testing and sensori-motor skill learning show that the effects of practice are generally advantageous even though the explanations of why this is so may vary. There is also ample evidence to suggest that what is done before practice in the way of thought and explanation can affect the results of the practice. There is apparently no evidence at all to imply that practice is not an inevitable part of motor skill acquisition. If this is so the way in which practice periods are utilised becomes a most important teaching point in physical education. As Stroud [122] has pointed out, practice does not necessarily make perfect. If undertaken badly, indeed, it need not lead to improvement at all and may even lead to retrogression. The important point here, however, is that practice is an inextricable part of motor skill learning. We must now turn to a consideration of how to practise in the most effective way.

The P.E. Teacher and the Management of Economic Skill Learning*
A considerable proportion of the physical educationist's time
is spent on skill instruction. That it is desirable for this time to
be spent in the most profitable manner goes without saying.
Given a specific amount of time, however, there remains the
practical problem of how best to use it. Fortunately, a good
deal of research has been done on learning and much of it is
pertinent to the acquisition of physical skills. It is beyond the
scope of this book to discuss at length the theoretical explanations of these findings for there is, at present, no general
agreement about them. Rather we shall give guidance along
lines which have been found to be empirically successful. The
following procedures seem to be particularly helpful.

DISTRIBUTED PRACTICE. Various studies, including those
by Knapp [123], Cozens [124] and Scott [125], point to the
greater effectiveness of distributed practice over massed practice
in motor skill learning. That the utilisation of brief rest periods
is especially valuable at the onset of motor learning has been
shown by Bell [126]. A study by Travis [127] indicates too,
that, in general and depending upon the nature of the task,
longer rest periods must accompany longer periods of practice
if optimum learning is to be achieved. The advantage of
distributed practice over massed practice is that, leaving aside
the factor of fatigue, it appears to give the organism a greater
opportunity to adapt itself. Bartlett [128] put it this way:
'in order that any complex series of body movements should be
given a fair chance to be consolidated or organised, very
persistent and prolonged repetition should be avoided'.
What actually constitutes the best possible distribution of
time for any one task must ultimately depend upon such
things as the individual's ability, fitness and motivation.
In attempting a summary we can do no better than quote
Knapp [129]: 'it may be said that, from the point of view of
skill learning, a short period of intense effort and attention is
better than a half-hearted longer period. Quality of practice
rather than quantity is required. At the beginning frequent

* For a more technical treatment of a number of the topics touched
upon in this section, see A. T. Welford's article, 'Acquisition of Skill' in
Readings in Physical Education, by J. E. Kane, Physical Education Assn.,
1966, pp. 1–27.

periods of shortish length seem advisable but when the foundations have been laid practices can be longer and less frequent.'

WHOLE-PART LEARNING. Both Johnson [130] and Hilgard
[131] agree, after examining the literature on the 'whole' and
'part' methods of presentation, that generally speaking it is the
whole that is the more advantageous. This is particularly
noticeable in subjects that are, compared with their fellows,
more 'intelligent', more mature, and more practised in whole
learning.

The real problem for the teacher is in deciding how big the
whole is to be.* In attempting to teach a head spring, for
example, is the physical educationist to persuade the pupil to
attempt the whole movement first time or approach the skill
through unit progressions? The chances are, as every experienced teacher knows, that if a complex sequence such as this
were tried the attempt would not only be unsuccessful but the
pupil would probably hurt himself into the bargain. Clearly,
where there is risk of fear or injury, in trying to teach by
'wholes', the approach is not to be recommended. Instead,
common sense dictates that part progressive learning is
necessary not only in order to build the neuro-muscular co-
ordination but courage and confidence with it. In skills where
there is no premium on danger it may be necessary to break a
complex skill down into smaller practiceable units so that it can
be better comprehended. In this context, Cross [132], after
experimenting with the teaching of basketball to 15-year-old
boys, comments: 'probably the practice of the parts proved
most valuable as much because of the simplifying of the intellectual concepts, as because of the simplifying of the motor
co-ordination'. If the parts are extracted from the whole for
purposes of practice, as it is sometimes necessary to do, it is
usually wise to reintegrate them back into the whole as soon as
it is feasible. If this is not done there is the danger that the parts
of the skill will remain inharmonious elements of the whole.

* M. V. Seagoe has attempted to rationalise the problem of 'wholes' by
making three statements: (1) they should be isolated and autonomous,
integrated units; (2) they must have 'form' quality; (3) they must be more
than the sum of the parts; they must be rational structures within themselves.
From 'Qualitative wholes: A re-evaluation of the whole-part problem'
in *Journal of Educational Psychology*, 27, 1936, pp. 537-45.

In the case of swimming, for example, as Niemeyer [*133*] has shown, an isolated practice like kicking is only useful in so far as it helps in the overall sequence of skill and when it forms a smooth cadence with the rest of the body's actions. The same is true of games skills. It should be remembered they should be related to the needs of the game and not regarded as an end in themselves. In this connection Rogers [*134*] has suggested that no teaching of 'part game' skills should be undertaken until pupils have been exposed to the whole game and recognise that there is a need for them.

Despite the considerable amount of material that pertains to the study of the effects of whole and part learning in general very little of it is to do with the skills that are the special concern of physical education, and as a result any conclusions come to must necessarily be tentative ones. What evidence there is seems to point to the following findings:

1. If a skill can be profitably taught through the whole method it should be done so as the pattern of movement remains complete. Such an approach is quite easy when teaching simple skills like throwing and catching, forward rolls and hitting a hockey ball.

2. In more complex skills like a flip flap or shot putt it may be necessary and desirable to break them down into smaller component parts, so that they can be better understood and more effectively practised, besides reducing the risk of injury or psychological disturbance. If this is done it is advisable to relate the selected units back into the skill or game from which they come.

3. Since what constitutes a manageable whole or part will vary from one individual to another the teacher must try to develop an insight into the pupil's capabilities—both mental and physical—so that, if and when parts are extracted from their wholes, this may be done in a way which will give the maximum help to the person undergoing the difficulty.

COMPREHENSIBLE GUIDANCE. One of the most important tasks in teaching is to present material in the clearest possible way. If there is uncertainty or confusion in the pupils' minds learning will be adversely affected. In the field of motor skill learning the following approaches have been found to be helpful:

1. Demonstration. A good demonstration is useful in two

ways. It widens our understanding of what is required by utilising our visual mechanisms and presents a standard to which we can aspire. Imitation in skill learning as in social learning has its effects as every experienced teacher knows. Experiments with films by Priebe and Burton [135] and Lockhart [136] point to the fact that the use of demonstration enabled the onlookers (the experimental group) to be more advanced than those that were not present (the control group) in skill acquisition appertaining to the high jump and bowling respectively. In a further study to do with gymnastics Brown and Messersmith [137] remarked that by using students to demonstrate the students became more highly motivated. My own experience would support this comment. Although some evidence does exist to suggest that demonstration has helped little, if at all, it is rather at variance with the majority of work done in this field which clearly points to its beneficial effects.

2. Manual or artificial assistance. It is not uncommon for physical education teachers to help a pupil with a movement with or without the aid of apparatus. It may be legitimately argued that support of this kind may not be of use in getting him to do things for himself and in some cases this may prove to be right. In other cases, (the majority in my experience), however pupils are led forward in the confidence that somebody is there to assist them to achieve something and in the knowledge that if anything goes wrong they will go away unhurt. In the teaching of a backward somersault, for example, an able boy can quickly learn the movement and have confidence to perform it if he is helped at the right time by a flick of the legs and some support in the small of the back. In the swimming bath too, as Kinnear [138] has shown, the use of floats can give a new joy and stimulus to learning. If not for mechanical reasons then for psychological ones it seems that manual assistance can be conducive to skill learning.

3. Verbal exposition. The difficulty of verbal guidance is that there is no guarantee of it being understood in the way the teacher intends. In this sense verbal comprehension may be said to be a function of intelligence and therefore plays a part in skill learning. In an experiment by Goodenough and Brian [139], for example, the phrase 'being careful' meant various things to the participants and this in turn affected their approach in tackling the skill set. The point is that unless

instructions are simple and well understood, they may prove to be more of a handicap than a help. Attempts to create a language of movement have not yet been entirely successful but in the approach by Metheny and Ellfeldt [140], where they use the terms kinaestruct, kinaescept and kinaesymbol, there are new concepts which can be used with advantage by physical educationists. Even so the experiment by Goodenough and Brian, referred to above, and one of the few done in this field that relates very closely to the sort of task that one is confronted with in physical education, showed that verbal guidance was a help. Of the three groups involved group A received no verbal help after the initial instructions were given; group B were given verbal guidance throughout the experiment; group C were given explicit guidance in a known and tried method as well as receiving extempore advice. Among the findings of the experiment, which comprised twenty 4-year-old children in a ring tossing situation, were that the median gains for each of groups A, B and C were 36%, 66% and 92% respectively. However in view of the limited nature of the experiment it would be improper to draw any general conclusions. All that can reasonably be said is that it is probable that verbal guidance in skill learning can be a help although to what extent this is so is dependent upon the amount understood and the aptness with which it is given.

4. Reflection. It is a curious phenomenon of skill learning that quite often periods of inactivity are followed by a surge forward. Cozens [141], for example, in teaching the shot putt reports that learning which had been on something of a plateau before a three-week rest break continued quite noticeably in the period that followed. This has not been an uncommon finding in my own experience in such varied fields as swimming, gymnastics and athletics. It is almost as if thinking and learning has continued during the spells of inactivity. Such a belief is to some extent supported by Clarke [142], who found that with more experienced boys mental practice alone did act as an aid to physical skill acquisition. The important point here seems to be that reflection can only be of value if it is based upon some experience. Without it there would be little to reflect upon.

KNOWLEDGE OF RESULTS. In a variety of learning situations a knowledge of results has been shown to be of use [143].

In the first place they furnish information according to which mistakes can often be corrected. In the second place they make a task more interesting and so have incentive value. A boy, for example, who has practised hard at his discus throwing is likely to receive satisfaction and stimulus if he knows his performance is improving. In skills of this sort, which can be measured objectively, the task of providing the results is not too difficult. In other cases such as in dance, where the skills involved are not so easily subjected to objective evaluation, some indication of results can be conveyed through the teacher's appraisal and guidance. In skill learning it is not so much success that matters as furthering the intention as it was first conceived. Squash is a good example. Here, 'knick balls' win points. They can come by accident or assiduous practice. The player should only feel truly satisfied if one comes through a deliberate and intentional shot, for it is only upon such a basis that complex skills can satisfactorily be learnt.

TRANSFER OF TRAINING.* Two theories of transfer of training find support in experimental data. Each will be discussed in turn with motor skill acquisition in mind.

1. Transfer through identical elements. This theory is chiefly associated with Thorndike and Woodworth [144]. It suggests that in a new situation the learner takes advantage of what the new situation has in common with previous experiences. In an experiment by Munn [145], which involved flipping a ball on the end of a piece of string into a wooden cup, he divided his subjects into two groups. To both groups he gave 50 trials with the left hand. Then, while one group rested, he gave the other group 500 trials with the right hand. Each group was then given a further 50 trials with the left hand. The group that had the additional 500 right-handed trials improved by 61·14%; the other group, that had no additional trials improved by only 28·55%. The conclusion of the author was that 'the average amount of transfer due to practice with the right hand was, therefore, 32·59%'. Other evidence is not so positive as this. In fact there are cases known of negative transfer. It appears, though, on the balance of evidence I have

* For a more detailed exposition of 'Transfer' as it relates to motor learning, consult Chapter 14 in B. J. Cratty's book, *Movement Behaviour and Motor Learning*, Kempton, 1964, pp. 265–81.

to hand, that the closer one situation resembles another the higher is the amount of transfer to be expected. According to Bartlett [*146*], 'there is also some evidence that transfer is more likely to be made from the relatively difficult to the relatively easy than from the relatively easy to the relatively difficult'. Thus, if this is so, a greater amount of transfer could be expected by practising with 12 lb. shots and then changing to 8 lb. ones. Even though this may be true, my own experience suggests that learning is most efficient of all, in this respect, if the correct weight is used throughout the practice period.

The main point here for the teacher is that he should make pupils aware of similarities between skills and movements in the hope that some transfer will take place. As Knapp [*147*] says, however, 'the one certain fact which emerges from the hundreds of experiments on transfer is that transfer of training is not automatic and that positive transfer cannot often be predicted with certainty'.

2. Transfer through principles. Bearing upon the point made above about the desirability of awareness is the question of the application of principles to learning situations. It was Judd [*148*] working at the beginning of this century who emphasised their importance. He proposed that what makes transfer possible is not the objective identities between two learning tasks but the appropriate application in the new situation of the principles or generalisations learned in the old. Thus he showed that a group which had received instruction about the principle of refraction did better in shooting at a target 12 inches under the water than a group that had received no instruction. In another experiment conducted by Hendrikson and Schroeder [*149*], Judd's basic hypothesis was largely confirmed. In the field of physical education Judd's contention is still further confirmed. Mohr and Barrett [*150*], for example, have shown that when a group is taught to understand and apply mechanical principles to the performance of swimming skills their improvement is greater than a parallel group that received no such help. McCloy [*151*] is also emphatic in his belief that a thorough grasp of mechanical principles can considerably facilitate the transfer of them from one form of skill learning to another and cites as examples striking a ball, driving in golf and putting the shot. Certainly Dyson [*152*] has shown that mechanical principles are very much a part of

athletic events and a good teacher will not hesitate to point out their general application. By doing so he will perhaps provide more thought among the pupils themselves and this in itself may lead to greater interest in looking for relationships. As we saw earlier, however, transfer is not automatic, even when good possibilities for transfer exist. Any opportunities that do exist must be looked for and handled skilfully by the teacher.*

PHYSICAL EDUCATION AND SUBJECT INTEGRATION

In the opening chapter mention was made of the need for synthesis and of the opportunities in physical education for contributing towards it. This chapter has already shown how important the physical activity of child's play is as a medium through which the parent/teacher can educate the 'whole' child. This is usually very clearly appreciated by those 'general' teachers who work in our Nursery, Infant and Junior Schools. In the Secondary Schools, however, where specialism is more prevalent, there is a greater danger of becoming a 'subject' instructor rather than pupil educator. To prevent such an attitude developing it is necessary occasionally to remind ourselves that the pupil is not an inanimate compilator of knowledge but a person who has a mind which the educator should tender and cultivate along a course which leads towards maturity and integration. The physical educator, in pursuing this aim, no less than any other teacher with specialist training, must be constantly alive to the possibilties of linking his own subject with those of others. In attempting this, besides having a wide and related range of information himself, he needs a knowledge of what conditions are likely to be most conducive to transfer. Here the two theories, to which we have just made reference in the context of motor learning, can be of equal use in connection

* There is the danger of negative transfer taking place if the general principles are similar but the finer techniques are different, e.g. learning in one activity such as badminton adversely affecting learning in another such as tennis.

See Nelson, D. O., 'Studies of transfer of learning in gross motor skills', *Res. Quart.*, Vol. 28, 1957, pp. 364–74.

with other forms of learning. Unlike motor learning though, it seems that in more academic situations some degree of transfer is the rule rather than the exception, providing the intention is there and that good techniques and methods are used. Also, generally speaking, a greater amount of transfer can be expected from the more intelligent type of person than from the less intelligent. All in all it is clear that a good deal more can be expected of transfer in the intellectual realm of learning than in the physical where skills tend to be specific. It is therefore with more confidence that the physical educationist can turn to the other aspects of his subject in the task of bringing about transfer. Bearing in mind these few introductory remarks it is worth discussing how physical education can satisfactorily integrate with other subjects in the school curriculum.

It was Whitehead [153] who pointed out that there is no antithesis between liberal education and technical education if both are taught well and with vision. In the same manner there need be no artificial division between physical education and academic education, or between examined and non-examined subjects. It should be possible for all such contrived labels to be diffused into one if the educator's alchemy is of sufficient quality. Even if complete synthesis is never quite possible in education, the teacher should always be directing his pupils from a state of 'what is' to 'what should be'. A lot is dependent upon the teacher himself. 'The good physical educator', says Cowell [154], 'is both a scientist and a philosopher. He is interested in gathering facts from psychology, philosophy, mental hygiene, . . . As a philosopher, he enquires earnestly into the meaning of these facts and arranges them into some total pattern or configuration. He subjects them to a certain philosophical discipline. What he *does* educationally is largely determined by the outcome of this process.' What he achieves as a teacher is largely a result of what he has achieved with himself. He must first transmute himself into an integrated being if he is to act as a successful agent in the transmutation of others. In this task of bringing about synthesis in knowledge and experience it will be seen that intention has a part to play. The teacher must deliberately set out to attempt to relate his own areas of knowledge if he is to help the pupils with whom he works to do the same. Witty [155] provides some evidence that boys in particular respond well to teachers interested in sports. If this is so it places the physical educationist in an enviable position with regard to the furthering of integrated learning. In the first place, since most children have a natural interest in sports and games, he should be able to communicate with them more easily and by so doing establish many points of contact. In the second place, the fact that physical education is a non-examined subject allows him more scope for the bringing together of common ground between his own and other subjects. Let us pursue this second point further.

The laws of mechanics are as applicable in vaulting and agility as they are in athletics or diving. The teacher who does not make this point to those pupils or classes which have some grounding in mechanics is missing a golden opportunity of linking the abstract with the personal. Often the perhaps dull and desiccated formulations of the laboratory can be given new meaning and significance through joining them with activities with which pupils are more directly and practically concerned. Understanding, for instance, may be improved if a specific activity like a fly-spring is taken and analysed for its effective utilisation of mechanical principles or otherwise. Besides being a useful intellectual exercise it can lead to a better appreciation of technique. In the setting of the gymnasium, athletic track or swimming pool the blinkered physicist or athlete can be awakened to the possibility of new thoughts and connections. By being encouraged to look about he may be led to relate his knowledge with adjoining fields of learning more readily.

In helping to further integration the physical educationist should never be frightened of taking advantage of situations as they arise and making the most of them. As Dewey [156] said: 'We always live at the time we live and not at some other time, and only by extracting at each present time the full meaning of each present experience are we prepared for doing the same thing in the future. This is the only preparation which in the long run amounts to anything.' A unique opportunity cannot be recaptured. To illustrate the point I would like to recount an instance from my own experience. A group of intelligent but less physically able sixth form boys had arrived at my lesson and were still in animated discussion about the problem of determinism and free will in life. They were speaking in metaphysical terms and clearly had in no way associated it with their impending P.E. period. Their confidence and attention was gained by my making some contribution to the discussion. They were still more intrigued by my irreverent question as to how many of them had balance-walked along a beam at hole twenty. None had. How many of them had ever tried, I asked. None had, although all were capable of doing it at hole ten or below. I put it to them that none was incapable of doing it because of physical inability. What success they would achieve, therefore, would depend upon the amount of free will they chose to exercise. Put in this fashion they saw the task of doing a walking balance along a high beam as an intellectual challenge. Two-thirds of them passed it and were well pleased with themselves. A moment in time had been turned to physical and intellectual account and some measure of integration achieved.

In the regular round of the physical education programme opportunities occur for cross fertilisation with other subjects. Athletic training and fitness, for example, can be made to link up with the chemistry of muscle action; life saving can be related to the work of the heart and lungs in biology; circuit training progress charts can be constructed by calling upon mathematical knowledge of graph construction. If the necessary knowledge is not already to hand, a demand for it can arise from a concrete situation. This in itself can be a stimulus to learning and lead naturally to a contact with other subjects. The good physical educationist should not only look for opportunities of integrating old yet unconnected knowledge, but of initiating new situations that will prompt interest and fresh enquiry. A lesson centred around reptiles, animals and man, for example, can, as I have seen, lead to a study of evolution. Talk of the Olympics can lead to an interest in the ancient Greeks and the history of their civilisation. The failure of certain athletes in Mexico, I remember, once led to a geography project entitled 'Climate and Racial Characteristics'. Enough perhaps has been said to indicate that physical education is not necessarily the poor relative it is sometimes made out to be in the promotion of intellectual effort. In the hands of a good teacher it not only affords a medium through which integration can come but also acts as a flowing river from which new and communicating channels may be sprung.

It would be wrong to think of physical education only in terms of physical activity. There is a valid place for discussion, enquiry and explanation. As Cowell [157] has observed:

'Physical Education has often been long on activity and too short on understanding'. Integration in education is important and at times it may be more profitable in the P.E. period to clarify the mind than to exercise the body. Let me elaborate this by further reminiscence. A group of scholarship sixth formers I once had were so physically exhausted as a result of a host of athletic commitments that I decided to change the second of the two periods they had each week from a practical to a theoretical session. They were such an academically heterogeneous group that they could learn a great deal from one another. The 'physical' in education became a central theme and each pupil was asked to contribute towards it in the shape of a 20-minute talk in the light of his own interest or specialist knowledge. The underlying purpose of the different talks was to cohere and relate various fields of knowledge. The list of topics they chose sprang from their interest in either the sciences or the arts. From the former came talks to do with embryology, genetics, body build, growth and development, sex differences, nutrition, human efficiency and statistics. From the latter came talks to do with the Greeks, sport in Roman times, games in primitive cultures, education in Samoa, the cult of athleticism, eugenics, the psychology of exercise, health and philosophic values, and sex and moral standards. A considerable interest was aroused by these talks and in the ensuing discussions a good deal of common ground established.

The study of a single theme from many viewpoints can reveal relationships where none was previously suspected. Physical education is a widely embracing subject and impinges upon many areas of learning. By a skilled and deliberate exploration of the opportunities offered the teacher can help his or her pupils effectively to dovetail the subjects with which they are concerned (formally and informally) in a more integrated and personal way. If such a process is successful he will be helping to rectify one of the greatest misfortunes of the age—the inability to look upon life coherently.

BOOKS FOR FURTHER READING

Andry, R. G., *Delinquency and Parental Pathology*. Methuen, 1960.
Bartlett, F. C., *The Mind at Work and Play*. George Allen and Unwin, 1951.
Bilodeau, E. A., *Acquisition of Skill*. Academic Press, 1966.
Bowlby, J., *Child Care and the Growth of Love*. Penguin, 1961.
Cowell, C. C., *Scientific Foundations of Physical Education*. N.Y. Harper, 1953.
Cratty, B. J., *Movement Behaviour and Motor Learning*. Kimpton, 1964.
Dyson, G. H. G., *The Mechanics of Athletics*. U.L.P., 1962.
Hebb, D. O., *The Organisation of Behaviour*. Wiley, 1948.
Hunt, J. McV., *Intelligence and Experience*. Ronald Press, 1961.
Jacks, L. P., *Education Through Recreation*. U.L.P., 1932.
Johnson, G. B., 'Motor Learning' in *Science and Exercise of Medicine and Sports*. N.Y. Harper, 1960.
Knapp, B., *Skill in Sport*. Routledge and Kegan Paul, 1963.
Mellor, E., *Education through Experience in the Infant School Years*. Blackwell, 1953.
Metheny, E. and Ellfeldt, L., 'Dynamics of Human Performance' in *Health and Fitness of the Modern World*. Athletic Institute U.S.A., 1961.
Miller, N. E. and Dollard, J., *Social Learning and Imitation*. Yale University Press, 1941.
Piaget, J., *The Origin of Intelligence in the Child*. Routledge and Kegan Paul, 1953.
Ribble, M. A., *The Rights of Infants*. Colombia University Press, 1943.
Solomon, P. et al., *Sensory Deprivation*. Harvard, 1965.
Vernon, P. E., *Intelligence and Attainment Tests*. U.L.P., 1960.
Wall, W. D., *Education and Mental Health*. U.N.E.S.C.O. Paris, 1964.
Wiseman, S. (Ed.), *Intelligence and Ability*. Penguin, 1967.
Whitehead, A. N., *Science and the Modern World*. C.U.P., 1927.
Woodworth, R. S. and Schlosberg, H., *Experimental Psychology*. N.Y. Holt, 1954.

CHAPTER FOUR

THE EMOTIONAL ELEMENT IN PHYSICAL EDUCATION

THE EMOTIONS AND THE EDUCATIVE PROCESS

In the last chapter, in the discussion of the sensory basis of intelligence, reference was made to the effects of maternal deprivation on early (and later) upbringing. The physical neglect resulting from lack of motherly handling and attention, led, amongst other things, to emotional difficulties and from these, according to Bowlby [158], can spring psychic 'trauma' which sometimes lead to delinquent acts in subsequent years. Freud [159] too, stresses the importance of the emotional connotation in helping the infant/child to pass through his oral, anal and phallic stages of pregenital development. The physical, or sensory, and emotional elements, as both these writers make clear, are never far apart. Frequently the one is the normal accompaniment of the other. In fact, as Jersild [160] has observed, 'emotion' is simply a label denoting a vast range of psychosomatic states. Emotions, indeed, may be regarded as a natural part of our everyday living experiences. As Gesell [161] says, 'Emotions are not foreign intrusions; they are part and parcel of the unitary action system'.

Emotional expression, like other complex forms of behaviour, develops through the combined process of maturation and learning. Its development is characterised by a transition from non-specific to specific reactions. In the newly born infant there is an overall response to stimulation but as the infant gets older its responses become more and more differentiated [162]. As the years pass by, it seems that there is an emergent pattern to which both maturation and environment contribute. The teacher must try to understand the former, and do something constructive and educational about the latter. He must understand, for instance, that to inhibit an infant in his locomotor explorations is likely to cause him frustration [163]. At the same time, knowing that some emotional states like fear, for

75

example, arise out of a lack of physical skill [*164*], he should be constantly on the look out for such inadequacies and attempt to rectify them in a helpful and sympathetic manner.

The physiology of emotional states can be studied objectively, as they were by Cannon [*165*], and be found to be associated with internal chemical changes and with external muscular actions, as when somebody jumps with joy or runs in fright. The subjective or feeling side of emotion is perhaps less well understood although it is recognised as being more or less present. There is nevertheless enough evidence to suggest that what we feel about a thing, object or situation affects our reactions to it. In education this is important. Broadly speaking feelings may be divided into pleasant and unpleasant. Unpleasant feelings such as hate, fear and anger can lead to avoidance action or to forms of behaviour that are negative and disruptive in nature. Pleasant feelings, on the other hand, like love, affection and sympathy, can lead to on-going practices and forms of behaviour that are both constructive and sociable. The emotions are of obvious importance to the educationist. If they take the 'wrong' course they may lead to incomplete development and to various forms of maladjustment. If they can be encouraged along the 'right' course they should lead to a higher level of maturity and integration. This does not imply, however, that progress towards maturity and integration should involve a studied avoidance of unpleasant situations. This would be impossible even if it were desirable. Rather it means facing up to them in a realistic and purposeful manner. It is more a question of control than the repression of an excited state. In many primitive communities, for example, the initiatory ceremonies for pubertal boys requires of them control in the face of demanding ordeals. If they refuse to submit to them or utter cries of distress they are considered unprepared to receive full adult status. In our western civilisation entry into adulthood is not marked by an all important occasion so much as by a gradual transition in overt behavioural terms. Young [*166*], in making a study of this transition, has noted the following differences between immature and mature emotional behaviour. The differences are more in terms of degree than of kind. First, there is a marked improvement in the amount of frustration tolerance. Second, there is a decrease in the frequency and intensity of emotional upset. Third, there is less impulsive or explosive behaviour. Fourth, there is a reduction in the degree of self-pity indulged in. Fifth, and last, there are fewer signs of overt emotional manifestations. Helping children to acquire emotional maturity does not mean that their paths should be made smooth or that they should be encouraged to side-step challenging situations. On the contrary, it entails facing them. In fact Rennie and Woodward [167] have defined an emotionally mature person as 'one who accepts unpleasant facts, whatever their genesis, as concrete situations to be handled rather than hated'. In this respect the teacher, as a model with whom the pupils can identify, can help to make fear, frustration and hostility give way to confidence, trust and co-operation. His very example in times of stress and emotion can serve as a pattern to be emulated. It is, therefore, necessary that the pattern set should be a mature and worthy one.

Enough has been said to indicate that the emotional development of the child is very-closely related to his general health and his personality integration. The forms of expression he uses are frequently the concern of other people and if they are found objectionable he may be ostracised and made miserable. This may in turn affect his work in school as well as his relationships with others. The good and effective teacher can often prevent such chain reactions from arising by the control he exercises and by some timely individual guidance. The physical educationist, operating as he does closer to the biological frontiers than his colleagues, has many opportunities for exercising his influence in such an inflammable field as the emotions.

Many forms of emotional disturbance are, of course, not so apparent. Those which reveal themselves in such complaints as headaches, skin diseases and accident proneness, for instance, are more subtle and often stem from psychogenic origins. To these the unwary teacher may find himself unwittingly contributing. He must therefore, be on his guard and bear in mind when presenting testing tasks that: 'Individual susceptibility to emotional shock is markedly influenced by constitutional factors, by all that has happened from the moment of birth, by the immediate situation, and by the interpretation which the child comes to put on it' [168]. The idea of the conception of the whole child is never more justified than when dealing with his emotional life. So important a place is this aspect of personality accorded that White [169] has gone as far as to say that,

'Neither the disorders of the body nor the disorders of the world can be cured without reference to the problems of emotional adjustment'.

The teacher's job though is more than that of an integrator and socialiser. He is also an educator and this means that he should not only provide opportunities for the acceptable release of emotional tension but try to awaken an appreciation for and an interest in beautiful things and aesthetic experiences. Only by so doing can the teacher help fully in making education a personal and enlivening process. Humanity today needs more sensitivity as well as more resolution if it is to escape from conformity and apathy. Education, if it is to be prevented from becoming sterile, must draw upon the enormous potential of the child's emotional reservoir. This involves more than a classroom study of art, music and poetry. It means coming face to face with nature and the full employment of the senses and body. This cannot be fully realised without reference to physical education. Perhaps Meredith [170] was getting at this when he wrote, 'When dressed as near naked as convention allows, in the gym, in the swimming pool, on the sports field or best of all among rocks, rivers and trees, he (the child) can be made aware of what it means to be alive. As he absorbs the sensations of air and water and grass, or rain, wind and snow, of sand and sea, of hills and valleys, he can learn not only to belong to nature but to make nature belong to him. He can re-establish this organic bond which our de-vitalised civilisation has done so much to destroy.' Macmurray [171], writing much in the same vein, claimed that, 'the fundamental element in the develop-ment of the emotional life is the training of this capacity to live in the senses, to become more and more delicately and com-pletely aware of the world about us, because it is a good half of the meaning of life to be so'. Experience through the physical senses is the basis of aesthetic thought and action and the initial promptings are probably 'caught' rather than 'taught'. By arranging and encouraging outdoor activities and by taking trips abroad to ski and to climb, the physical educationist can do much to promote such promptings.

Jersild [172] has observed that 'a child's emotions influence his perceiving and thinking'. If this is so the influence can be for good or bad. Even though this is generally realised, little is done in boys' schools to educate the emotions other than in an academic and pedantic manner. In the Grammar Schools particularly, too much time is still devoted to the desiccated demands of the examination syllabus. This not only hinders the development of balanced personality but also affects academic standards. This neglect of the emotions in some schools was well expressed by Murray [*173*], thirty years ago. He said: 'We leave men's emotions to the mercy of quacks and charlatans and we educate people as if they were amenable to logic only. . . . If we exalt right thinking over right feeling we are sure to get astray even from right thinking.' It could be added that what we feel about the ideals we hold strengthens their import and personalises their value.

Clearly when other subjects are more strongly tied to the classroom or workshop and in consequence are more 'mindful' in their approach to the education of feeling, physical education with its undefined programme, has an unrivalled advantage.

In a society which has failed to synchromesh our emotions with our religious life, some other means must be found to give them the freedom and direction they require. The physical educationist can play a significant part in this liberation process not only by bringing the child closer to his natural surroundings in the way we have suggested, but by capitalising upon his impulsive desire to play and to imagine in the school situation. Whilst play, as a part of physical education, has already, frequently enough, been turned to good account in the Primary Schools, its spirit is less in evidence in the Secondary School stage partly, no doubt, because of maturational factors but also, I believe, because of the exalted position written work has come to have. It is somewhat ironic to find that, at a time when ballet, Russian dancing and the muscial have never been more popular, the body as an instrument of emotional and aesthetic expression is relatively neglected in our educational system. Whilst the woman physical educationist has done much to redress this imbalance in the last few years (and has perhaps given it too much emphasis within the framework of her own programme), her male counterpart has barely begun to recognise that for boys there is a similar need for creative expression. Perhaps they fail to see as a corollary of this that bottled-up emotional energies or their improper release can be as detrimental to good health as organic unfitness.

Because it is the best possible 'subject' for balanced

psychosomatic expression, physical education is also the best medium for the education of the emotions, for they will be blended with the other aspects of personality and be synthesised into the harmony of the person. Play and dance are the best examples of this process.

PLAY AND EMOTIONAL DEVELOPMENT

Axline has said that play is the child's natural medium for self-expression [174]. It is this, yet at the same time it is more than this. It helps in the development of the self; it helps acquaint the child with reality; and above all it helps in the process towards self-realisation and integration. Play is everything to the child and he reacts totally to it. The cognitive, conative and affective aspects of his mind are all absorbingly engaged by it. He matures and he learns. He 'assimilates' and he 'accommodates'. The child's emotional development is inextricably bound up with the other factors of his being. Because of this it is necessary that the whole gamut of his life is taken into account and given direction if the emotions are to be educated. Play in the 'planned environment' enables the teacher to do this without obtruding too strongly into an educative process which is essentially child centred and self-initiated. Play in the company of a helpful and sympathetic adult not only helps the child to learn, it helps him also to adjust both socially and emotionally—the two are very intimately linked. The unobtrusive guidance of a teacher in children's play activities can go a long way in satisfying those basic needs about which Thomas [175] speaks—security, recognition, response and adventure. In fact the characteristics of play—freedom, imitation, repetition, make-believe, activity, seriousness, satisfaction and spontaneity—have a good deal of common ground with these basic needs. The unconscious wishes or needs are, so to speak, 'lived out' in play experience. The same may be said of the emotions. Emotions are a part of the child's life and there is a need for them to be expressed. Play provides a medium through which they can be naturally expressed. This is beneficial on two counts. Firstly, it permits the externalisation of a feeling, which according to the psycho-analyst, is good for the child's mental health. Secondly, it enables the teacher to give comfort and guidance in times of trouble. By being present and alert, and by dealing with the child's emotional problems tactfully as they arise, the teacher can educate them at the same time. The teacher's role is an important one, but before dwelling more upon his professional leadership in this respect, let us look at the function of play in the child's emotional life.

The Function of Play in the Child's Emotional Life

Play is prophylactic to the child [*176*]. It gives him an opportunity to release such feelings as frustration, insecurity, fear, bewilderment and confusion. As Axline [*177*] comments: 'By playing out these feelings he brings them to the surface, gets them out into the open, faces them, learns to control them, or abandons them. When he has achieved emotional relaxation, he begins to realise the power within himself to be an individual in his own right, to think for himself, to make his own decisions, to become psychologically more mature and, by so doing, to realise selfhood.' In exterialising destructive feelings like hate and aggression he prevents them from corroding his inner self. In whatever form they are expressed they lead in the short term to relief and independence and in the long term, with skilful guidance, to socialisation. Animosities and tensions in the young child are not altogether under control and play acts as a safety valve through which they can pass without fear of punitive action. The free and permissive atmosphere that should accompany the child's play does not, however, infer that the teacher does nothing. On the contrary, unless he helps children to come to terms with themselves and other people, play would have only a limited cathartic value. Play should also provide a means whereby the child can resolve his own problems. In the same way that psychiatrists get their patients to talk out their problems so the teacher can often help children to play out theirs. Conflicts can be solved through an appeal to the imaginative content of play. One such instance, I recall, was of a boy of seven who was fearful of standing on a beam and swinging on a rope to a mattress positioned eight or ten yards away on the gymnasium floor. Nothing would persuade him to attempt this feat until mention was made of Tarzan and crocodiles. This transported him not only into an inspired state of mind but served as a spur to action, which led him to swing safely from the 'river island'. Afterwards he was so delighted with his success that he repeated this challenge many times over and soon became quite confident in his own abilities to do this and similar tasks.

Not all attempts, however, lead to success. Sometimes they lead to disappointment. If the real problem is temporarily too much, feelings of anxiety or a sense of failure can be softened and later overcome by an illusory or make-believe mastery. This escape into phantasy not only ameliorates his recognition of himself as a 'poor' individual but serves to prepare himself anew for a more mature and determined attempt later. Success in the child's phantasy life in solving an emotional problem often helps him to meet the real situation successfully at a later stage. The make-believe exploration of an attractive self-image, reinforced by the teacher's encouragement and suggestion, can turn a tide of failure into one of success [178].

It seems almost as if play acts as a catalyst in this two-way emotional shunt. As Freud [179] once observed: 'Children tend in their play to repeat everything that has made a great impression upon them in actual life whether pleasant or unpleasant, so they thereby abreact the strength of the impression and make themselves master of the situation'. Whether success ultimately comes or not, play in conjunction with the teacher's assistance can help the child to adjust to both his inner and outer world. He must learn to accept both himself and others if he is not to become an emotional victim of his shortcomings.

So far play has been discussed only as a vehicle for the resolution of emotional problems. Looked at in this manner it can be regarded as a form of preventive medicine. In addition it may serve as a medium through which the teacher can inject feelings of happiness and well-being. To do this the teacher needs to create a friendly atmosphere in which activities can be pursued. He needs also to take notice of the movements and ideas in which the child is interested. If the circumstances of the environment are right, the teacher or play leader should find that there is an abundance of opportunity to promote feelings of joy and pleasure. Playing pirates, for example, not only provides strenuous activity and adventure but a good deal of satisfaction and fun besides. If laughter and humour can be associated with exercise and learning, there is a greater chance that education through the physical will succeed. Gesell [180] has said of humour that it must come 'through suggestion, atmosphere and experience'. The same may be said of a number of other wholesome feelings and responses. In this enlivening and expansive process the physical and imaginative content of play can help enormously in the cultivation of a rounded person. Qualities like sympathy and compassion, for example, can be encouraged and empathetically felt through the make-believe situations that play engenders. Some idea of the vast overall importance of emotional attachments in education was conveyed by Hadfield [181] when he said: 'The first object of all education, intellectual as well as moral and religious, is the formation of right sentiments and dispositions—i.e. the attachment of emotions to the right objects, ideas and persons'. In this endeavour the play leader or physical educationist can contribute considerably if he has the will and understanding to do so.

Play, Psychotherapy and Physical Education
Some indication has been given of the way in which play acts both as a safety valve and as a resolver of conflicts. It can also serve as a mirror from which the child reflects his innermost strivings and emotional difficulties. It is in this sense that the psychiatrist has come to look upon play as a diagnostic tool. He looks upon it not only in this way, however, but also as a means by which treatment can be administered. Play is both diagnostic and therapeutic. Authorities like Axline [182] and Jackson and Todd [183] have been very clear as to how play can help in each respect. Children, absorbed and unaware in their play activities, reveal themselves just as usefully to the physical educationist. Although he is by no means a therapist he often finds himself unwittingly acting as one. Many aspects of his subject merge with play and even where they do not situations arise where personality is seen to be in action. As was said earlier, the physical educationist is nearer to the biological frontiers than most of his colleagues and he is able to see at work the basic forces of child nature. In physical education, observes Cowell [184], 'Weaknesses and strengths are readily spotted. Physical cowardice, sissiness, fearfulness, or nervousness becomes evident. Here teachers get a much more adequate view of personality in action than can be obtained from the narrow confines of the clinical laboratory, the classroom alone,

or "paper and pencil" tests purported to measure personality. Furthermore the informality of the student-teacher relationship in physical education and athletics is of unusual value for effective guidance.' All this being the case it puts the physical educationist in a similar position to the play therapist. He is there, not only to promote activity and to develop skills, but also to comfort, to guide and to help in the modification of certain forms of behaviour. However there are some important differences in approach. Whereas in play-therapy complete freedom is usually given to an individual child, in physical education play is always likely to be subject to general educational striving and indulged in in groups. Even so there is a fair amount of common ground between them. They both require active participation; both aim to help the child to adjust; and both give opportunities for showing responsibility.

Play, whether therapeutic or educative (or both), is basically a creative function of child behaviour and it is with this idea in mind that the function of dance will be examined.

THE SIGNIFICANCE OF DANCE IN EDUCATION

J. S. Mill [185] in his essay On Liberty wrote: 'Human nature is not a machine to be built after a model, and set to do exactly the work prescribed for it, but a tree, which requires to grow and develop itself on all sides according to the tendency of inward forces which make it a living thing'. Although most educationists would concur with this statement, it is a regrettable fact that our educational system (and society) pushes children more and more into a mould of conformity. This is particularly so at the Secondary School stage where they tend to do the same things, see the same things and learn the same things. This trend will no doubt be even more in evidence in future with the increasing use of mass media for instructional purposes. Even in physical education where the programme remains free of examination dictates, procedures adopted are sometimes in danger of following prescribed and furrowed pathways. However the good physical educationist, conscious of his task to help his pupils grow 'on all sides', will not rely solely upon the usual round of sports and games with their circumscribing rules and arbitrary standards, but will utilise also those aspects of his subject that recognise and permit creative and personal expression—movement education, mime and drama all have a valid place here. If dance is singled out for discussion, it is only because it incorporates many of the values that movement education, mime and drama contain.

Educational Values

Dance as a medium of self expression is nothing new. Indeed it is very old. Several examples of early Magdalenian art testify as much. So too, do the discovered remains of such past civilisations as the Egyptian, Babylonian and Assyrian. In ancient Greece dance frequently formed a part of large ceremonies whether in connection with the Olympic Games or the religious festivals at Delphi. Even today there are several extant primitive communities that exemplify this age old form of expression.

The story of dance, running as it does through history, makes it seem as if it forms a part of the essential mode of man's existence. At one time fresh and vital, it dwindled with the evolution of civilised society and became more and more sterile. This change was recorded by G. Stanley Hall [*186*] who wrote at the beginning of the present century: 'We have in the dance of the modern ballroom only a degenerate relic, with at best but a very insignificant cultural value, and too often stained with bad associations. [How topical this sounds.] This is most unfortunate for youth, and for their sake a work of rescue and revival is greatly needed, for it is perhaps not excepting even music, the completest language of the emotions, and can be made one of the best schools of sentiment and even will, inculcating good states of mind and exercising bad ones as few agencies have power to do.'

It is perhaps no accident of history that just as men were getting desperate for their own individuality and conscious of their own inability to express themselves Isadora Duncan should appear in America and re-discover the natural and expressive function of dance and disregard the stylised and stereotyped procedures that had been acquired with the passing of the years. The seeds she planted later developed into the movement known as Modern Dance.

Since 1948 when Laban [187] first published his book, *Modern Educational Dance*, a great deal has been spoken and written about the subject and many of its most ardent supporters have seen in it the panacea of education's ills. However, despite the sometimes fanciful claim made on its behalf, it is an important factor in education in general, and physical education in particular, if talk of balance, individuality and personality integration is to have any meaning at all.

Perhaps Laban himself was most sensible of its contribution to the adolescent when he said: 'In schools where art education is fostered, it is not artistic perfection or the creation and performance of sensational dances which is aimed at, but the beneficial effect of the creative activity of dancing upon the personality of the pupil'. It is often upheld, and with justification, that physical, mental, social and cultural benefits accrue as a result of being taught dance, but M.E.D.'s pre-eminent contribution to the development of the personality of the adolescent is that it keeps alive the springs of spontaneous action and provides a vehicle through which it can be freely expressed. In making this provision dance is able to serve as a medium through which emotional feelings and difficulties can be liberated and resolved in much the same way as they were in childhood through play. However, this does not do M.E.D. full justice. In addition it has the comprehensiveness to become the most perfectly balanced synthesising instrument of the educational workshop. Havelock Ellis [188] must have had something of this all-embracing quality of dance in mind when he wrote: 'Dancing is the loftiest, the most moving, the most beautiful of the arts, because it is no mere translation or abstraction from life; it is life itself'. In a more analytic way but getting at the same thing, G. Stanley Hall said [189], to quote him once more, that 'right dancing can cadence the very soul, give nervous poise and control, bring harmony between basal and finer muscles, also between feeling and intellect, body and mind. It can serve as an awakener and a test of intelligence, predispose the heart against vice, and turn the springs of character towards virtue . . .' What other branch of school education can appeal to all aspects of personality more harmoniously and more fully and in a more balanced way, all at the same time, than dance? Education is after all concerned with the development of the whole person and in M.E.D. physical education has a force which facilitates the concurrent involvement of the thinking, feeling and acting aspects of the pupil's personality. In this it is unrivalled.

Although M.E.D. is often undertaken in pairs and groups and thereby serves a socialising function it is more importantly, perhaps, a personal and subjective form of expression. At its best it avoids the structured, formalised and stylised forms of approach and gives opportunity for inventiveness and creativeness to which the more traditional forms of physical education do not lend themselves so easily. In this imaginative freedom dance has something in common with painting, music and poetry, and, like them, it finds that true freedom can only come through a self-imposed rather than a super-imposed discipline. It has the advantage over these other arts, that it enters into a more evenly represented psychosomatic relationship. In most forms of artistic expression the body is very much the junior partner. An adolescent who is unable to express himself satisfactorily through his paint-brush, keyboard or pen may find that he is able to do so more readily through his body. Dance provides a further opportunity of exploring his own potential and of becoming more completely aware of himself as a person and as an individual in a climate that does so much to stifle it. It is no less than a contribution to what Maslow [190] calls the process of 'self-actualisation' or a move in the direction of what Reid [191] is talking about when he speaks of 'self-activity' and 'personal living'.

Another value in dance is that sometimes some of the more subtle and gentle of emotional responses can be awakened and cultivated through the experiences it can provide, especially when it is accompanied by music. This is no bad thing in a world that trades so much upon hate and violence. What the adolescent is unable to articulate about he is often able to feel and empathise with, and if dance can help boys and girls to become more appreciative of, and sensitive to, the people and things around them then certainly it is fulfilling an educative aim. As Nunn [192] has said: 'The central duty of school teaching is to encourage loves. . . . It follows also that the first step in teaching any subject should be to lay the firm foundations of love.' If a love for dance is encouraged this may in turn lead to a love of the values for which it stands. This can only be to the credit of physical education and of benefit to the personality.

Mental Health Values of Dance

Much of what is written about dance in the school situation is unsupported by experimental findings and has to be taken on trust. In a number of mental hospitals, however, more objective studies have been made that illustrate the mental health values of dance. Bender and Boas [193], Chace [194], May [195], and Rosen [196] speak of personality changes resulting from participation in dance programmes and make certain observations concerning the patients' improved state of health. Layman [197], in summarising these and other findings, suggests that dance is a potential medium for mental hygiene because it has the following characteristics:

1. It provides a channel through which the individual uses rhythmic movement for the expression of feelings, desires, conflicts, drives, fantasies and defences, thus providing possible release of tension through catharsis, and promoting greater spontaneity.

2. It is a non-verbal means of communicating with others, and so assists the individual to relate to others and identify with others.

3. It helps the individual to acquire poise and confidence in social situations.

4. It is creative and elicits reactions of approval from others and so gives the individual satisfaction in achievement.

Layman goes on to make the comment, which is worth noting, that some people are able to express themselves more fully in a relatively 'structured' form of dance than in a 'creative' one where they have greater freedom. This is no doubt true, but the fact remains that in modern dance physical education has an expressive medium that is of unique educational significance.

OTHER FACTORS ABOUT PHYSICAL EDUCATION THAT HELP WITH HEALTHY EMOTIONAL DEVELOPMENT

In addition to the considerable influence play and dance can have in the emotional development of the child and adolescent there are certain other factors about physical education that can make a contribution to the emergence of the personality.

Promoter of Physical Skills

Jersild [198] reports that an important cause of fear among children arises from a lack of physical skill and that the development of such skills results in the elimination of fear. Clearly the physical educationist has an important function to perform here. By helping the child to learn to do things for himself he can assist him in his general development a great deal. By teaching him how to swim or how to dive, for example, the physical educationist not only helps the child to dispel his fears of the water but gives him a new confidence in his abilities and a better image of himself.

Physical skills and accomplishment are socially important to him and unless he is reasonably proficient at them he may be unwanted by the group and as a result suffer from feelings of rejection.

Eschewer of Rigid Criteria

In certain forms and branches of education feelings of inadequacy often arise because children are compared with one another or because they are measured against an imposed and arbitrary standard. Although physical education is not altogether free of this it does try to alleviate such repercussions by providing media which are not open to these objections. In movement education, for example, it is the best of which the child is capable that is required, not a rigid and inflexible standard. And because it offers more scope for the imagination than some of the more traditional activities it is, to some children, more likely to bring pleasure and satisfaction, especially to those who are not very successful at such activities as vaulting and agility.

It should be added, however, that even in movement education, despite there being no fixed criteria, a child can sometimes become conscious that he is unable to jump as high or stretch as far as another and, if this occurs, it can lead to feelings of inferiority, inadequacy and frustration. This state of affairs can be alleviated, if the teacher considers it desirable, by the formation of groups based upon approximate abilities. Such a scheme seems to have several advantages. In the first place the emotional problems about which we spoke are more likely to be removed by work being done in more compatible sets. Secondly, programmes more suited to the group's needs and abilities can be worked out. Thirdly, homogeneous groupings in movement education as in other branches of physical education, can lead to the teacher doing his work more effectively as he does not have to contend with big variations in ability.

Medium for Self-actualisation

For the child who has failed to distinguish himself in other spheres of school life physical education may be a godsend. Success at cricket or soccer may give him the recognition he needs and the enjoyment that goes with it. It may also provide a type of expression about which we have not yet spoken but which according to McCloy [*199*] is 'found in physical competition, the desire for mastery, for self assertion, the desire to co-operate loyally with others of one's group, to express one's ego in leading others, in adventuring, in sheer physical striving, in feeling physically adequate, and in the joyous perfection of movement'.

Agency of Adjustment

In the realm of emotional adjustment physical education can sometimes play a part. To illustrate this point I would like to quote two case studies from my own experience.

Case A involves a boy who, owing to a thyroid deficiency, was of diminutive size. At fifteen he was only 4 ft. 8½ in. in height and 5 st. 12 lbs. in weight. As a result of these proportions he was ragged, teased and bullied. He never went under. The treatment he received made him determined to outdo his fellows.* In 'gym' periods he tried very hard and showed courage and perseverance. In many activities he could outshine many of his larger and more naturally gifted classmates. Physical education became a means whereby he could demonstrate his equality. So powerful was his motivation that his apparent inabilities were turned into positive strengths. His relative success became marked and with it came recognition

---

* The tremendous effort made by this boy is very much in keeping with Adler's theory [*200*] of overcompensation, where in an attempt to deny a weakness, the weakness becomes a goad to superior performance.

by the staff and his classmates. This gave him status and acceptance. As a result he became less 'edgy' and easier to deal with. He became a more balanced individual.

Case B concerns a boy aged thirteen with a paralysed arm. He was protected and molly-coddled at home, had played no games and was physically weak. At school he was fearful of physical situations and felt inadequate and inferior. With the passing of time he learnt to swim, play basketball and tennis. He participated in cross-country runs and circuit training. He grew stronger, more skilled and assured. His confidence and self-image greatly improved. He not only became a more capable person but came to accept his disability graciously. His efforts and successes were admired by his fellows. Whereas previously he was teased because of his religious mania and derided because of his feeble tearfulness, he now became accepted by the group and was respected for his convictions and self confidence.

In each case it cannot be claimed that physical education and its activities were solely responsible for these emotional re-adjustments but it is certain that they helped a good deal.

Aid to Rapprochement and Discussion
Physical education has an advantage over many other branches of education in that it encompasses many more different and informal occasions. In the hills or on the rivers a different slant on a boy or girl can often come to light that will bring about a new insight into his make-up. In the free and easy atmosphere of the fell walk or camp site, difficulties and concerns are often brought up and freely discussed, whereas in a more formal setting, where the rapprochement is not so pronounced, they might go unvoiced and undiscussed. In situations like these the physical educationist can talk over and around a variety of topics with his pupils and perhaps in doing so bring about a better quality of relationship besides being able to make suggestions and give guidance. In such circumstances, where there is time, inclination and a mutual respect that induces a 'talking out' of problems, a form of group therapy may be said to exist. It is not so dissimilar to those that serve this very purpose in clinics both in this country and in the United States.

BOOKS FOR FURTHER READING

Axline, V. A., *Play Therapy*. Houghton Mifflin, 1947.

Bowley, A. H., *The Natural Development of the Child*. E. & S. Livingstone, 1957.

Bruce, V., *Dance and Dance Drama in Education*. Pergamon, 1965.

Doubler, M., *Dance: A Creative Art Experience*. Univ. of Wisconsin Press, 1959.

Ellis, Havelock, *The Dance of Life*. Houghton, Mifflin, 1923.

Freud, S., see a *Primer of Freudian Psychology* by C. S. Hall, Mentor Books, 1960.

Gesell, A., *Youth: The Years from Ten to Sixteen*. Hamish Hamilton, 1956.

Jackson, L. and Todd, K. M., *Child Treatment and the Therapy of Play*. Methuen, 1948.

Jersild, A. T., 'Emotional Development' in Carmichael's *Manual of Child Psychology*. 2nd Edn. Wiley, 1954.

Jordan, D., *The Dance as Education*. O.U.P., 1938.

Laban, R., *Modern Educational Dance*. MacDonald & Evans, 1948.

Langer, S., *Feeling and Form*. Routledge and Kegan Paul, 1953.

McCloy, H. C., *Philosophical Basis of Physical Education*. Appleton-Century-Crofts, 1940.

Meredith, G. P., Personal Education article in *P.E.A. Year Book*, 1964-5.

Phillips, M., *The Education of the Emotions*. Allen and Unwin, 1960.

Reid, L. A., *Philosophy and Education*. Heinemann, 1962.

Rogers, F. R., *Dance: A Basic Educational Technique*. Macmillan, N.Y., 1941.

Russell, J., *Modern Dance in Education*. MacDonald & Evans, 1958.

Sachs, C., *World History of the Dance*. Norton, 1937.

Symonds, P. M., *The Dynamics of Human Adjustment*. Appleton-Century-Crofts, 1946.

Wooten, B. J. (Ed.), 'Educational Values of Dance' in *Focus on Dance II, A.A.H.P.E.R.*, 1962.

Young, P. T., *Motivation and Emotion*. Wiley, 1961.

CHAPTER FIVE

THE SOCIAL ELEMENT IN PHYSICAL EDUCATION

PHYSICAL EDUCATION AND SOCIAL ADJUSTMENT

It is generally conceded that social behaviour is largely determined by the culture and by the particular circumstances in which people are brought up. Social adjustment involves being able to integrate successfully with others. In this process play is of considerable importance to the child.

Social learning, like other forms of learning, is a product of growth and development. As the child matures so, owing to the joint forces of heredity and environment, his social responses alter.* This gradual transition of the child can be followed in his play groupings. Gesell [201] gives this picture of sequential change:

1 year	Shy with family group. Shy with strangers.
18 months	Solitary play. Not ready for play with other children.
2 years	Likes to be with other children. Parallel play. Not ready for co-operative play or for extensive group activity.
2½ years	Beginnings of co-operative play. Chiefly parallel play and imitation. Little sharing.
3 years	Some spontaneous group play. May be quite harmonious. No distinction between sexes in play.
3½ years	Group activity, but some members of group may discriminate against others and forcibly exclude them.
4 years	Co-operative and imaginative group play—sustained dramatic or imaginative play. Tendency in play for division along sex lines.
5 years	Children mostly in play groups of two: seldom more than five in a group. Imaginative play gives

* For a discussion of this topic see N. L. Munn's *The Evolution and Growth of Human Behaviour*, Harrap, 1962, Chapter 15.

appearance of being co-operative though actually involves little real co-operation. Each child carries out his own individual ends and has little concern for the group as a whole. Children symmetrically organised in play, ready for all relationships.

6 years   Much group play. Groupings flexible. Little concern for welfare of group. Little solitary play.

7 years   Group play primarily for individual ends. But beginnings of real co-operative play.

8 years   Child enjoys group activity. Accepts the fact that his role in the group is to some extent determined by his abilities and limitations.
Real co-operative play and carrying out of simple projects. Not yet ready for complex rules, but can accept very simple ones, or directions. Boys and girls separate off in play. Prefer play with the same sex.

9 years   Children like to act as a group and compete as a group. Accept own role in group and can evaluate contributions of others. May be more interested in success of group than in own individual enjoyment. In games or for projects, organisation is complex and detailed, co-operation is excellent.

It will be seen that in this progress from solitariness to co-operative endeavours, play has not only reflected the child's unfolding maturity, but has acted as agent in bringing about social adjustments. In helping the child to become increasingly socialised the parent/teacher can assist a good deal by permitting him the proximity of other children so that he can learn by being with them and following through the stages rather in the manner outlined. To deprive the child of play-friends is to undermine a necessary part of his development. In a sense, of course, social adjustment begins to take place from the moment a child is born. The handling and attention he receives from both parents, as was shown earlier in connection with intellectual development, is of equal importance in his social upbringing. From his parents he learns many things which later affect his social behaviour. As Jeans [202] observes: 'Attitudes are communicated to the infant from the earliest moments and reflect his behaviour'. A great many child studies have indicated as much and, while the influence of the parents is of obvious importance in the social development of the child, our concern here is more directly to do with the way in which play, as an aspect of physical education, can assist it. In speaking of play it is important to remember that the parent/teacher, acting as he does as a controller, guide and mentor, can help enormously.

Social Adjustment through Play

According to Cowell [203]: 'Health, strength, and physique determine to a great extent what, and especially how, a child plays. Play skills, in turn, are of major importance in companionship and friendship in the social relationship of children.' If this statement is true, it is clear that the physical element in the educative process is of great significance in the contribution it makes to the child's social adjustment. To a certain extent there is a reciprocity here. The child becomes healthy through play and conversely he socialises himself by indulging in it.

Play, as we have already noticed from Gesell's account, involves a gradual extension of contacts and as a result the child soon learns, if he has not before, that the 'I' in him is no longer completely autonomous. The attempt to impose his will on others will involve him in acts of aggression and hostility. These are a necessary part of his adjustment for through them he learns that other children have wills and rights of their own. So usual is this form of adjustment that Bridges [204] regards it not only as a normal stage of development but a necessary one. If he makes enemies with some of his playmates he will also make friends with others. The recompensing thing about having foes is that it often brings allies. 'The compensating value of this rivalry of groups,' says Isaacs [205], 'is that it brings to the children the active experience of mutual consideration and help within the group. They get the feel of working and playing together. They suffer the pressure of other people's wishes and contrary opinions which are yet not too different, not altogether contrary, since they come from friends. Each child's friendliness to his fellow-members of the group makes him more ready to give way to see their point of view.'

Throughout the child's development it must not be assumed that if he is just left to his own devices all will be well. There are times, of course, when the parent/teacher is best advised to let him solve his own problems. Although the over-anxious or over-protective mother, as Levy [206] has pointed out, can be of disadvantage to the growing child it seems desirable that some assistance is given. To quote Isaacs [207] once more: 'The notion that children must not be interfered with at all, but left to work out their own salvation, without control or guidance, is, however, seen to be without firm basis. In some directions, the child cannot do without our guidance. He needs the help of external restraints in learning to control and deflect his own impulses, particularly the aggressive ones.' The parent/ teacher has a considerable responsibility in watching over the play activities of children. There is room for both free self-discovery and for control. Judgement and discretion are needed. The good parent/teacher will know just how far certain forms of behaviour in play should be allowed to run before they are stopped. Many potentially damaging episodes can often be averted and even turned to good account by timely intervention and guidance.

The parent/teacher can also help the child grow to higher levels of social adjustment by the provision of equipment. Articles like boxes, crates, barrels, tubs, car tyres, planks, ladders and bricks often necessitate co-operative effort in order that children can manipulate and make use of them in their associative and imaginative play. This in turn often involves a good deal of speech. 'The give and take of conversation,' says Mellor [208], 'the interchange of ideas and the understanding and tolerance that these things bring, all contribute to the development of the child as a member of society.' As they go about their play together, she continues, 'they learn to respect other people's work and property; to share and to take turns; to organise, instruct and obey; to lead and to follow. They learn consideration for others. . . . They learn to modify their own strong desires in the interests of the group, and so accept the discipline of the group as a natural and necessary thing.'

As play continues throughout the period of childhood the processes of imitation and suggestion are at work. The inter-actions children undergo one with another help them to modify, adapt and adjust. Unless the parent/teacher is about to guide them into good and acceptable ways they might, because of a developing group loyalty and mores, dissent from the aims with which education is concerned. If social adjustment is controlled by an untutored group code, it is not necessarily compatible with what the educationist would call socially acceptable behaviour, or in keeping with the aims of good character development as we shall see later. The child is prone to, and influenced by, the teachings of his parent/teacher and his play group. It is desirable for the smooth advancement of his personality that the two should be in harmony. It is the duty of the physical educationist to see that ambivalent habits and attitudes do not arise especially in those situations where there is danger of him directing his main energies to the winning of games rather than to the playing of them.

When dealing with the emotions it was suggested that a satisfactory expression of them had social advantages. This can now be illustrated more clearly with reference to play. Hartley, Frank and Goldenson [209], for example, speak of integrating the troubled child into the social life of the group by means of dramatic play. They say it can act as a 'social cement' and induce the solitary child to move out of his seclusion. For the pre-school child, block play can often be a means whereby the newcomer and isolate can be brought into the group and its participations. About this they comment: 'The more complicated block projects lend themselves readily to group participation in which leaders may put aside personal demands and the unskilled or unwanted may find a place for themselves. Time and again we find a spirit of camaraderie that is rarely duplicated in any other type of play.' In the play of the music and movement lesson too, children may be seen to unfreeze and allow their inhibitions to melt away. In a section on music and social integration the same authors write: 'The shy, withdrawn child seems to have more vigour, more power, more ability to maintain contacts during music; the aggressive child finds in it a challenge to the exploration of his abilities, as well as an integrating agent that calms anxieties and opens the way to constructive relationships'.

Perhaps enough has been said to indicate that play, both for the pre-school child, who is experiencing emotio-social difficulties, and for the normally developing child of the nursery, infant and junior school, according to how it is provided for and handled, can have real and beneficial socialising effects. If one has doubts about the place of play in social adjustment one has only to look at the findings of researchers who have worked in this field. McKinney [210], for instance, after reviewing evidence about children who have grown up with limited play and companionship says that they are less well adjusted than those who have been exposed to normal play life. He goes further and states the values of play to be as follows: (1) it increases social poise and spontaneity; (2) it develops independence; (3) it releases tensions; (4) it forms the basis for friendship, popularity and leadership.

Cowell [211], in another study, suggests that in the pre-adolescent stage of development the 'fringers' or those who do not enter very fully into the big-muscle play activities of the physical education programme, tend to have the following characteristics: (1) they are less socially acceptable to other boys and girls; (2) they tend to regard others as more acceptable than they are regarded by other boy sand girls; (3) they are considered much less able by other boys and girls to fulfil school positions demanding qualities of virtue than are the actives; (4) they show a marked tendency to exhibit those negative behaviour trends which psychiatrists, mental hygienists and clinicians indicate are symptoms of great clinical value. Needless to say many of the above points are value judgements imposed by the culture and by those who form the in-group. Even so the fact is that in terms of social adjustment and social acceptability the importance of the participation in play activities exists. This may be the fault of what 'is' as opposed to what 'ought' to be. For the present we must content ourselves with the observation that play is of great significance as a factor in social adjustment and because of this the physical educationist should be alert to its possibilities.

Participation, Skill and Physical Ability as Factors in the Social Adjustment of the Adolescent
In recent years there has been a tendency for sociologists and anthropologists [212] to look upon adolescence as a social phenomenon, but as Sollenberger [213] has pointed out, even when social influences are recognised in full measure there still remains the important fact of biological change and all that this infers. Nahapiet [214] gives some clarification of what is meant here when she writes: 'Important as bodily changes are, the effect of them on the young person's views and feelings about himself are even more significant, for physical development, as is well known, has a psychological effect on the

attitudes a young person has regarding himself and on the attitude others have towards him'. Whenever experiments have been conducted they seem to give support to this general statement.

It is probable that the coming of physiological maturity allied to the values of the culture in which he finds himself together conspire in the adolescent to provoke within him a high regard for physical ability and skill. Whatever the reasons, experimental findings show that they are held in considerable esteem and as a result occupy an important place in his social adjustment. In order to illustrate and clarify the point we shall look at and discuss a number of pertinent studies.

Investigations such as the one carried out by Lehman and Witty [215] on the recreational pursuits in young people between the ages of seven and nineteen show how strongly physical activities are represented and how these frequently form good bases for social interaction. For boys particularly, interests centring on the 'physical' remain well represented throughout the entire age range. In a later study, Cowell [216] largely substantiated these findings. He found further that the purposes students try to satisfy through participation in physical education activities tend to change with increasing maturity but in adolescence motivations like 'mastery of game skills', 'to have fun', and 'to learn to control myself and be a good sport' featured noticeably in both sexes. Other reasons such as 'to be with my friends' and 'to get along and understand others' were also given. Foehrenbach [217], working along the same lines, found that another incentive to after-school sports participation was 'to make friends'. It is clear from these and other studies that a good deal of social interaction centres around physical activities and the pre-requisite ability to take part in them. They not only provide a means by which young people can come together but serve as a vehicle through which the adolescent can be helped to social adjustment.

The study by Lehman and Witty, already referred to, implied that proficiency in activities like basketball and dancing enabled the adolescent to participate more fully in the group's social life and Jones [218] is more categoric when he says: 'Particularly amongst adolescent boys, the ability to take part in playground games and to play a normally lively role in the various physical activities is more often than not an important factor in the development of successful social relationships'. Later in the same article he goes a step further and says: 'It is chiefly amongst boys that physical abilities play an important part in social adjustment . . ., however, competitive athletic skills are amongst the chief sources of social esteem in the period preceding maturity'. This second statement is given further support by Biddulph [219]. In comparing the personal and social adjustment of 50 high school boys of high athletic achievement with that of 50 boys of low athletic achievement and evaluating adjustment on the basis of teachers' ratings, a sociometric technique and the Californian Test of Personality, he found that students ranking high in athletic achievement demonstrated a significantly greater degree of personal and social adjustment than did students ranking low in athletic achievement. Oliver [220], working with educationally sub-normal boys in England, reports that 'the highest relationship was found between social development and the physical abilities' in his investigation.

Other physical characteristics also play their part in affecting the social adjustment of the growing adolescent. Strength, for example, with which physical education can have so much to do, has considerable social significance. In connection with this, Jones [221], in another study, says that the 'positive relationship of strength to "prestige traits" (among boys) . . . may be regarded as evidence of the role of physical prowess in the adolescent value system. Superior strength is a part of a complex of physical characteristics valued highly in the pre-adult culture; the absence of these characteristics is a handicap which can be overcome only by strongly compensating personal traits in other areas which are also highly valued'. In yet another study [222] by the same author comparisons were made between the 10 strongest and the 10 weakest boys in an urban school population involving 5 high schools. Adjustment was evaluated by means of the California Reputation Test and cumulative records. 'The summary for the 10 boys high in strength', he says, 'indicated a tendency for strength to be associated with a good physique, physical fitness, early maturing, social prestige and social stimulus value, and an apparently satisfactory level of personal adjustment. Similarly, the 10 boys low in strength showed a pronounced tendency towards an asthenic physique, late maturing, poor health, social difficulties and lack of status, feelings of inferiority, and personal maladjustment in other areas.'

Although the various findings to do with physical education and adolescent adjustment, such as the ones presented above, seem well nigh irrefutable, they must not be accepted uncritically. In the first place it does not follow that these studies, which were largely based on American youth, are equally applicable to the youth of this country, although what evidence there is in the United Kingdom [223] does suggest that the pattern is by no means dissimilar. In the second place what may be said of adolescents in general is not necessarily true of an adolescent in particular. As Jones [224] observed, there may be other factors besides physical prowess that enable an adolescent to integrate himself successfully with his peer group. The playing of a guitar, for example, can bring this about. There may be a difference in outlook between one group in society and another with regard to the nature of the physical pursuits and the form of value placed upon them. Certainly the picture presented by Mathew Arnold [225] of the Barbarians, Philistines and Populace in nineteenth-century England would suggest this and it is not unlikely that even today, despite the increased democratisation of sport [226], disparate responses would emerge. In this country an upper class adolescent, having perhaps attended an independent progressive school, is not necessarily going to have the same values and attitudes about physical abilities (or for that matter a number of other things) as an adolescent from a working-class home who has attended a local secondary modern school. Even in the U.S.A., where youth is apparently not so hidebound by social distinctions [227], this would no doubt apply though perhaps to a lesser extent. Individual, class or societal differences affect the place and importance of physical attributes and skills, but they remain of considerable social significance to the average adolescent in our culture and they feature prominently in his relationship with his peer group and therefore in his concept of 'self'.

Developmental and social psychologists agree that adolescence is a period characterised by a struggle for emancipation from adult control. At this time acceptance by the group becomes a matter of special significance. As Horrocks [228] says: 'the peer group is one of the greatest motivating forces of adolescence. The relation of an adolescent to his peers and his participation in their activities is usually one of the most important things in his life. His ego-involvement is often such that exclusion can be a major tragedy, while acceptance brings feelings of security and happiness.' Because physical activities and abilities feature strongly in adolescent pastimes and values they carry with them a good deal of social status and esteem within the group situation. Brace [229], in showing a marked relationship between athletic ability and social status in boys in the age range of 13 through to 16, shows this quite clearly.

Coleman [230] too, in examining sports and studies as paths to success in the adolescent sub-culture gives further evidence in support of the same contention. He gives a number of experimental findings which are relevant to the present theme. In answer to his self-posed question: 'What is the relative status of the boy who is only an athlete, the one who is only a scholar, and the one who is both?', the following discoveries were made:

1. 'The athlete/scholar far outdistances all others. In total choices as a friend, as someone to be friends with or be like, and as a member of the leading crowd, the average athlete/scholar receives over three times as many choices as the average scholar who is not an athlete, and over one-half times as many as the average athlete who is not a scholar. The boy who is neither athlete nor scholar receives little recognition and respect, an average of only one-seventh the number of choices received by the athlete/scholar.' Although the athlete/scholar does better than anybody else in the adolescent value system it is noticeable that:

2. 'The pure scholar fares far worse than does the pure athlete. He is mentioned as someone to be friends with or to be like only about a third as often as is the athlete.' The pure athlete constitutes 5.3% of the boys' student body, but gets 30·5% of the be-friends-with and be-like choices, and 24·8% of the leading-crowd choices. The pure scholar constitutes 5·5% of the student body, receives 12·7% of the be-friends-with and be-like choices, and 11·9% of the leading-crowd choices. It will be seen that scholarship alone receives less than half the recognition and respect from peers than does athletic achievement alone and yet these, together with the small athlete/

scholar category of 1·3%, are held in considerably more esteem than the rest of the student body put together. It is worth noting here that: 'The athlete in every case outdistances the scholar, as the scholar outdistances the student body as a whole. . . . The athletes most outdistance the others in being named as the most popular with the girls. . . . Overall it appears that athletic stardom stands highest as a symbol of success, . . . as a means of entry into the leading crowd, as a way to gain popularity with the girls, and as the man with the most friends.'

All in all it is clear that physical ability is of real significance in the adolescent value system. Though Coleman's findings were based upon American youth with whom the athletic cult is particularly strong and in this country they may not be quite so sharply differentiated they would, no doubt, follow the same overall pattern. Although it has been demonstrated that it is possible to gain social acceptance and esteem through physical prowess it does not follow that this course is open to everybody. It is open only to the gifted few. The physical educationist should remain aware of this and not expect too much from his less able pupils. If he has concern for the social adjustment of all his pupils he should concentrate more on getting them to participate wholeheartedly in the activities of the programme rather than on equating success, by implication or otherwise, with high achievement. As an educationist he might even have to damp down the ardour of acclaimed athletic success for the good of its recipient as well as of its donors. Physical education, with its group activities and its association with physical abilities, holds within its grasp tremendous potentiality for helping each and every pupil to a greater degree of social adjustment and welfare.

CHARACTER AND PHYSICAL EDUCATION

The Meaning and Place of Character in our Society
The last section showed that the social adjustment processes contingent upon the activities with which physical education is concerned are both formidable and influential. It is necessary that the pupil should be with and get along with other people,

for as Murphy [231] says: 'The young child or the adolescent "finds himself" in a group. It is in the group that one realises oneself as a personality.' There are attendant dangers though on accepting the group's standards, attitudes and opinions without question for, from the ethical standpoint, they can be either good or bad. Social development then, especially if it involves a passive conformity to group mores, is not necessarily in accord with the values for which education in our society should stand. Character, in the sense that I intend using it, is a term which helps bridge the gap between what often 'does occur' as opposed to what 'ought to occur'. It is to do with the culture's values and yet at the same time allows for will and independence of thought. It is, according to Jones [232], 'the sum total of the attitudes and overt ways of behaving of the individual which are the correlatives of his regulative habits, developing values, and volitional drives. It is a dynamic concept involving inner creativeness and psycho-cultural determination.' It is to do with personalised and independently thought out goals. But this is a mature state of affairs. The child, as in all educative undertakings, must be helped and guided. Until such time as he is able to exercise independent thought and judgement of his own, it is better that the parent and teacher should introduce him to values which are generally agreed to be 'right' for western democratic society. These come to us largely through the classical philosophers and the Christian tradition [233]. It is better that values should be taken from such a source than from the possibly 'wrong' codes of an ephemeral peer group.

Education should see to it that social development proceeds hand in hand with character formation. Ideally they should be in one and the same 'experiential continuum'. One of the main concerns of education is the development of character and it is only right that it should interest itself in the direction it should take. The following socially orientated qualities should be fostered: kindness, unselfishness, friendliness, truthfulness, justice, honesty, thoughtfulness, courtesy, helpfulness, tolerance, cheerfulness, loyalty, co-operation and a general consideration for others.

If the teacher is in agreement about the desirability of these qualities for his pupils, it becomes necessary for him to get them established within the group's code of behaviour. Since these qualities are generally recognised as worthwhile in our culture they will, if commonly adopted, according to Toulmin's thesis [234], make society as a whole more 'socially cohesive'. But education must do more than just make society mechanically efficient. If it stopped at that it would reduce the qualities mentioned above to a number of cogs in the wheel of socialisation. The educationist must aim to present such qualities as values to be not only upheld but thought about, felt about and willed into being. In the group situation they should act as beacons to which members should look and towards which they should strive. They should become dynamic and personalised forces characterising a group's inter-personal relationships. They should be more than procedural formalities; they should be made to incite a comprehensive involvement of the personality rather in the way elaborated upon by MacMurray [235] in his Gifford Lectures.

Of course, character is more than a limited number of social traits all of which are personalised and willed into being. It is also to do with independence of thought and action. The two sides of character—independence of thought and action and an acceptance of a social mode of conduct—need not be mutually exclusive. Individual qualities like courage, ingenuity, initiative, decision, perseverance, determination, self-reliance, self-control, self-restraint, thoroughness, enthusiasm, reliability and resourcefulness are also generally considered to be desirable and the teacher should try to get them to live within the group situation so that they become a part of its dynamic functioning. Without traits from both sides of the coin of character it is doubtful if people like William Wilberforce and Elizabeth Fry would be produced to keep our society progressive. The one side gives due deference to the best of the culture's social values; the other, due expression of the right of the personality to think and to act independently, and yet remain within broad limits of conformity.

Character Development in Physical Education

So far the discussion has been confined to the question of what character is. We must turn now to a consideration of how many of the qualities to do with character can be fostered.

A great many educationists and psychologists have stressed the importance of early and continuous training in the development of character. Current evidence [236] suggests that there is no age at which the child suddenly becomes responsible although it is worth recording that Piaget [237] has shown that moral training in children can be linked with their level of maturation. He claims to have distinguished between two forms of morality. The first is confined to early childhood and is a type of egocentric behaviour and is characterised by a tendency to follow rules because they are handed down by elders. At this stage of development Piaget could find nothing within the child upon which he could build a desire to do this or that because of any 'mutual respect of child for child'. This is roughly in accord with the picture presented by Gesell [238] of early social responses of children in play groups, discussed earlier. He found that the second type of morality originated later in the life of the child than the first and was motivated by a desire to change the rule in a game if in its working a play-fellow was not treated in the way he himself would like to be. This we can regard as an indication of creativeness as opposed to conformity in the development of character.

If the matter of maturation is important to character educa-tion in relation to play activities, so too is the question of con-sistency. The child should always be presented with, and com-mended for, a worthy pattern of behaviour. Praise for a good deed is satisfying and often emotionally charged and the laws of learning and conditioning are as true for good acts as they are for bad. Habits and attitudes are laid down early in life and even though they may not be understood and personalised at this stage they form a necessary part of effective character formation. This does not mean of course that what the child learns in his early days he is inevitably committed to thereafter. On the contrary as Jones [239] explains: 'Ethical concepts and behaviour are continuously in the process of formation and revision throughout life, of course, but the earlier a child is oriented toward desirable conduct and generalisations, the earlier does he begin to internalise the controls upon him and to evolve his own sense of relative values'.

The next general observation from which the physical educationist can profit is one to do with generalisation and transfer. The fact that he may be consistent, for example, in his insistence upon honesty in the playing of tennis doesn't necessarily mean that because honesty is adopted in these particular circumstances it will be adopted in other situations in general. In fact the studies by Hartshorne and May [*240*] have shown the reverse to be true—that specifity of traits tends to be the rule rather than the exception. Therefore it follows that the physical education teacher in concert with his colleagues should aim to offset this tendency by trying to bring about the generalisation of good qualities by applying them in accordance with the rules of transfer about which we have spoken earlier. This is a problem which goes far beyond the province of the teacher or the school. It requires joint cooperation from all the institutions of the community which are concerned with the character development of children. The physical educationist, however, can make a useful contribution in furthering this cause.

Having considered these general points it is worth looking in more detail at the way in which physical education can best help in the development of character.

PHYSICAL ACTIVITY. Throughout this discussion emphasis has been placed on the distinction between intellectual acceptance of a form of behaviour and the putting of it into practice. The exercise of the will has been constantly stressed. The activities with which physical education is concerned call for real decisions in real situations. They are not hypothetical; they are actual. The touch-judge whose team is drawing and who sees the winger of his team score a try after he has put his foot in touch is left with a choice of whether or not to put up his flag. He must make a decision and he will be forced into a position of acting truthfully or untruthfully. It is hoped he will make the right choice, in keeping with what he knows to be correct. It is no academic nuance. It is a test case of practical application. As Kilpatrick [*241*] says: 'We cannot build a response without responding. . . . Situations reported in books and elsewhere afford but a colourless and unreal responding. A little is possible. A child may say "If I ever get a chance I'll do thus and so". This has some effect but such effects are slight in comparison with actually responding to actual situations.' Neumann [*242*] elaborates upon this same point still further. He writes as follows:

> The most important moral agency, when it is rightly inspired, is found in the actual performance of the pupils themselves. It is one

thing to hear right conduct praised or see it exemplified; it is quite another, and more necessary thing, for boys and girls themselves to do the acts. Character is essentially a matter of action, the habitual performance of certain kinds of deeds rather than others, and the only genuine way of learning how to do these deeds is to do them, just as the only way to learn tennis is to play it.

In physical education, because of the social and live decision-provoking situations it engenders, education has a distinctive character-forming force which, with careful handling, can be for the good.

GROUP DYNAMICS. Many of the activities with which physical education has to do involve groups; option groups, ability groups, activity groups, teams for games and so on, all fall into this general classification. If they function for a period of time their members are likely to fall prone to what the social psychologists call group behaviour. Briefly speaking, this is characterised by 'norm' formation, which means that group members come to assume standards and forms of attitude and conduct representative of the group. Thrasher [243] and later Sherif and Sherif [244] have shown the great power of the group to mould the behaviour of its members. Because of this it is particularly important that the physical educationist should inspire, by whatever sound methods he can, the adoption of the sort of qualities which we have ventured to set down. In this he can be successful and that improvement can take place in character formation is verified in an experiment conducted by Jones [245]. In the face to face interactions of games like basketball, soccer, hockey and rugby, 'norms' are quickly formed and it is essential that they should centre around qualities like enthusiasm, co-operation, loyalty, honesty and fairness if character formation is to be assisted in the way that educationists would like it to be. If there is some truth in the assertion that some moral good comes of simply playing games because of their intrinsic nature, it is perhaps still more true to say that a still greater good is likely to come if such activities are used as a medium through which to teach the qualities which have been mentioned in this section.

In order that the physical educationist should be under no illusions about the immensity of this whole task, it must be said that most of the objective information available on character formation in physical activities is disappointing in its findings on the general effects of transfer [246]. This, however, is true of nearly all other teaching situations. The real problem in effective character building is being able to expose the child to the same influences over a prolonged period of time whether he be at home, school or in the streets. If the physical educationist can be successful within his own sphere, and by shaping group 'norms' he can do influential work, he can play a real and effective part in the general endeavour.

OPPORTUNITIES FOR CONCOMITANT LEARNING. Physical education, because of its manifold and multifarious activities, offers unusual possibilities for concomitant learnings. The teacher should always be on the look out for these so that he can capitalise upon them. By way of illustration consider a number of attendant learnings that can come about as a result of a child participating in a group activity concerning the high jump. The list below is based upon the one given in Mitchell and Mason [247]:

1. Considerate or inconsiderate of others: in putting up the bar or not doing so after knocking it down, in smoothing the pit or not after jumping, in starting the practice with the bar low or high for poorer jumpers, in keeping quiet when another man is to jump or in making noise which will disturb him, in taking unnecessary time in jumping or in jumping promptly.
2. Selfish or unselfish: in waiting his turn or seeking to jump out of turn, in insisting on keeping the bar near his own jumping height or adjusting it to the needs of others.
3. Tolerant or intolerant: towards poor jumpers, towards smaller boys, towards others he does not like, towards other racial groups represented in the team.
4. Reliable or unreliable: in attending practice regularly, giving his best in practice, doing assigned duties in connection with practice.
5. Fair and just or unfair.
6. Obedient or disobedient.
7. Loyal or disloyal.
8. Self controlled or lacking in self control.

9. Modest or boastful in victory.
10. Persevering or quick to surrender.
11. Courageous or cowardly.
12. Prompt or tardy.
13. Profane or refraining from profanity.

It will be seen that all these points carry with them a dual possibility. It is to be hoped that the teacher would actively encourage the desirable alternative in each of the above cases and always be alive to the possibility of doing the same with others like them. Indeed, if the teacher is to be professional in his approach he must remember his work is as much to do with the bringing out of good qualities as it is with physical skills and organic fitness and therefore take advantage of all situations that help bring them about.

PROMOTION OF DIRECT AND CHALLENGING EXPERIENCE. It will be recalled that when we were dealing with the emotions that one of the basic needs, according to Thomas [248], was the need for adventure. Evidence that such a need exists comes from a variety of sources. All too often its satisfaction is met vicariously through the comic, the television, the film, the magazine and the novel. Vicarious adventure involves no risk; direct experience does. It is because physical education provides this latter sort of experience that it is valuable both to the individual and to society. Trevelyan [249] recognised this when he wrote: 'Without the instinct for adventure in young men any civilisation, however enlightened, and any state, however well ordered, must wither and wilt'.

Although it would be possible to cite many instances in physical education where qualities like resource, initiative, determination, perseverance and loyalty are required it is perhaps away from the facilities and organisation of the school that the greatest challenges are made. In situations such as those provided by Outward Bound courses, the sea and the mountains become the forces with which the individual is confronted. Here he is faced by the realities of nature and it is in first-hand encounters with them that 'the full capacity of the will is revealed and a new standard of effort and conduct achieved' [250]. Both physical and moral courage, if it is possible to split the two, are at a premium. Courage does not come by wishing. It comes completely only by the act of doing. In the open spaces one learns not to avoid fear but to live with it. The knowledge that one can live with one's self is a dear possession indeed. In a society that in some ways is over-protected, physical education offers, in its outdoor activities particularly, the experience of a struggle with nature. From such a brush the first seeds of real maturity can be sprung. Young [251], the scholar mountaineer, was perhaps getting at this when he wrote: 'It is when physical strength and endurance have been tried to their utmost that we become sensitivised to beauty, and aware of deeper emotional possibilities in ourselves'.

If there is a marked absence of proof in educational literature about the matters raised in this section, it is perhaps partly due to the fact that some of the concepts involved (what is loyalty for instance?) are somewhat elusive and difficult to measure objectively. The educationist must not be put off by the un-imaginative scientist who claims that if a thing exists it can necessarily be measured. 'Statistical analysis', observes Cowell [252], 'should be the right hand of, not the substitute for, insight.' Rather the educationist must work in a spirit of well-founded faith. To those who have seen the reality of these processes it will perhaps be comfort enough for them to know that they operate even if they cannot at present be objectively verified.

Finally no matter how favourable the circumstances of up-bringing and experience the ultimate in a person's development lies within himself. Children should be led to realise that they are actively engaged in helping to shape their own destinies. Many of the qualities presented here are demanded in the never ending struggle of lifting our standards from one level to the next. It is never easy. The difficulties of self-improvement should never be underplayed. As Williams [253] has so eloquently put it:

> We do no service to youth if we give the impression that excellence is easily come by, that there is no correspondence between ends and means, or that words can substitute for deeds. Youth should know that fine character does not come easily but rather that the great traditions of mankind are wrought out of a struggle, sacrifice and suffering. Personal effort not circumstance produces the excellent man.

COMPETITION: APPRAISAL AND GUIDANCE

Competition, unlike co-operation, does not necessarily involve the presence of others. One can, for example, compete against oneself or against a set time or standard. For the present purpose however the term will be used within the context of social development.

Research by anthropologists such as Mead [254] suggests that competition is not nearly so pronounced in some cultures as it is in our own. Amongst Zuni Indians, for example, it is barely known. Instead of competition they stress co-operation and non-aggressiveness. This is evident in their workaday round as well as in their religious life. Our culture, by way of contrast, aids and abets competition and at the same time, somewhat paradoxically, encourages co-operation. It is certain in any event that in our western democratic society the amount of competitive behaviour increases with age [255]. Murphy [256], indeed, has shown clearly enough that the concept of competitive self-enhancement is almost normal by the age of four. Maller [257] confirms this. In an experiment with school children he found that self-motivation was very much more strongly represented than group-motivation. When conditions were so arranged that the children could choose between the two forms of motivation it was shown that in 75% of the choices self-motivation was preferred. Several studies [258] make it clear that by the time children reach the Primary School stage a good many of them have already learned that doing things better than others is one way of gaining approval and prestige. The importance of the role of imitation in social learning is put convincingly by Miller and Dollard [259] and it seems very likely that a good deal of the child's competitive behaviour and outlook comes to him through imitating the competitive behaviour of others. The parent/teacher would do well to remember this if he wishes to influence his child away from an excess of it or alternatively encourage it to a greater degree.

A good illustration of how two cultures can have fundamentally different attitudes to the same game is given by the

Midcentury White House Conference on Children and Youth [260]. It said: 'the children of the Hopi [American Indians] took to basketball enthusiastically, but could not be taught to keep score. Competition did not interest them but they loved the teamwork. Our own children, trained to value fair conflict, need the competitive score to give an incentive and spice to the game. They can be taught teamwork, only incidentally and in a framework of competition.'

There seems little point in educationists trying to ignore the prominence competition has in our way of life particularly as it is bound up with the very qualities and processes which it is felt necessary to foster—independence, determination and self-actualisation, for example. Perhaps Russell [261] was speaking more in this cultural sense when he said: 'Competition and co-operation are both natural human activities and it is difficult to suppress competition completely without destroying individuality'. Even so, natural though competition may be, it does not necessarily mean that it should be deliberately cultivated as an incentive in education. The school does not have to follow the lead of the adult world. There are times when it should set the standards rather than follow them. Which teacher, for example, would want to promote the sort of degrading competition that centres on the Smiths outdoing the Jones in material possessions? The point is that competition is of itself neither good nor bad. It can, however, sometimes result in good or bad. This is true no less of competition in physical education than in any other walk of life. If the physical educationist knows the full potentialities of competition in his sphere of work, he will be better able to use it wisely in the pupil's healthy psycho-social development.

Advantages of Competition
In the first place there is little doubt that competition is effective as an aid to motivation. It is well known to every physical educationist that competition is a stimulus to effort. In the Primary School such phrases as 'Who can jump the highest?' or 'Who can stretch the furthest?' evoke a far greater response than a bald command such as 'Swim as far as you can'. Rivalry is a great spur to learning. Several studies [262] have shown that, regardless of the activity, children tend to learn more rapidly in situations where competition is involved than where

it is not. 'Experimentally then,' as Breckenridge and Vincent [263] observe, 'we can say little against competition and rivalry as methods to be used in motivating children.' Effective as competition may be as a motivating technique, it cannot be adopted *ad lib* without reservation because an excess of it can militate against some of the social qualities which have been mentioned and which are also to do with learning and education. Even so, as Isaacs [264] has said, 'It is not, however, helpful for the teacher always to be teaching the doctrine of co-opera-tion and to admit no ethical value in rivalry. It is one thing to condemn the wholly bad practice of using the motive of com-petition as a spur to intellectual effort (e.g. by moving children up and down in class, according to their achievements in arithmetic, etc.) and quite another to rule the motive of competition out altogether as a spontaneous element in children's social relations.' Competition, especially with young children, should be used as a joyful spur to action and arise out of their willingness to co-operate. As soon as it becomes an imposed and unwanted device it can lead to possible dangers the nature of which are discussed below.

Competition can also act as an incentive to participation. As we saw earlier, particularly in the case of the adolescent, there is a positive desire to be accepted as a member of the group. Physical prowess, because it stands high in the adolescent value system, is one way of gaining admission to a group. Com-petition provides the means by which one can show one's physical worth either by successfully competing with another individual who is already respected or by gaining a place in a representative team. In no small degree athletic ability is bound up with matters like prestige, status and popularity. It is partially because the adolescent is aware of this that he is drawn to compete and make his bid for social acceptance. Over and above this there are, according to Klein [265], more subtle forces to do with competition at work. She writes: 'The impulse to give evidence of his courage in the real world and the desire for competition with others become more prominent. This is one of the reasons why sport, which offers so much scope for rivalry with others no less than for admiration of their brilliant feats, and which also provides a means of overcoming anxiety, plays so large a part in the adolescent's life and phantasies.'

Almost inherent in the question of group competition is the question of group co-operation. It is virtually inconceivable that one group should compete against another without some agreement about the role each group member is to play. In soccer, for example, each member of a team will take the field knowing not only what his own function and duties are but what the functions and duties of his colleagues are besides. Only on such a basis can understanding and teamwork flourish. When a group has a common objective, as Sherif and Sherif [266] have shown, it tends to cohere and bring about an increased amount of interaction and integration. It can, at its best, bring about a sacrifice of the self to the group endeavour. Such an ideal lies at the heart of why many educationists prefer team games to individual ones. If co-operative and sportsman-like striving is not outweighed by the desire to win at all costs then competition far from being socially destructive can in fact be socially enhancing.

Competition in games involves submitting oneself to the rules that control it. This, if properly put over, should not only lead to their ready acceptance as they stand but to a willing interpretation of their spirit. Only if this double act of socialisation is made manifest can the educative process be said to take place. In writing of fairness, Cerf [267] elaborates upon this theme still further. He says:

> Fairness is a sense of justice and the rights of men even in fields where these rights have not been codified and where breaking the rules does not bring about punishment by society. The fair man voluntarily sticks to the rules and agreements of the game, gives his adversary the same rights he claims for himself, shows consideration for the weak, and accepts in good spirit the foibles and fortes of his team-mates. Fairness brings about an instinctive appreciation of the rights of man, of the sacredness of mutual obligations, of justice and tolerance, and the discipline of co-operation—all of them virtues basic to democracy.
>
> The true habit of fairness is competitive teamwork. Sports have always had the function of training men in fairness. There is no reason why the method of competitive teamwork should not be carried over from the playground to the classroom.

If to the average physical education teacher the above is not more than a romantic idyll, it is perhaps because he has not striven hard enough to see and to do something about bringing competitive teamwork towards such a possibility. The norms of groups are created not discovered and the teacher should be constantly trying to influence them in the direction of Cerf's idealism.

Disadvantages of Competition

Competition in physical education has from time to time been criticised on the grounds that it is close to hostility and that it often induces states of emotional tension that can lead to personality disturbance. It is true, as Johnson [268] and his co-workers have shown, that in the periods preceding athletic competition emotional change can and does take place and that this change can be measured by a variety of techniques. His general impression, after looking at several forms of sport, was that 'the "disturbed state", which so commonly characterises the pre-contest situation is probably not detrimental to individuals who are comparatively free of profound personality disturbances' [269]. It may be that the neurotic adult or the unstable child is placed under relatively more tension than the normal child and that the tension induced in them does not subside so quickly after the competitive situation is over. By and large evidence seems to suggest that the normal child can cope without undue disturbance with a normal amount of competition. The abnormal or nervous child on the other hand, may become over anxious and placed under severe stress. If this is the case there is good reason for giving him consideration and special dispensation. However as Williams [270] observes: 'Educational policy for a general practice, however, cannot be derived from the limitations of emotionally abnormal children. Such children should have the supervision in activities that their special problems require, but they are the special cases that illustrate the principle of individual differences.'

Hostility and aggressiveness, always noticeably present in the young child, appear to reassert themselves in adolescence. Wall [271], for example, writes: 'It is probable that the increased energy of the sex drive itself (in both sexes) at least in the early stages, reinforces aggressiveness and accounts in some measure for the unruliness, difficult behaviour and even delinquency which is a marked feature of the period between 12 and 15'. The question that concerns us, bearing in mind this developmental tendency, is whether competition fans this antisocial form of behaviour or whether it gives it scope for sublimatory expression? There is very little research evidence on which to base any firm conclusions, although it is worth recording that a study by Johnson and Hutton [272] found a noticeable decrease in the aggressive tendencies of wrestlers the day after competition. My own experience and observation would support this 'after effect' of strenuous competitive exercise. Even whilst exercise is being taken, providing the teacher is in firm control, there is no reason why hostile feelings should be converted into offensive acts. A study by Kahn [273] supports this. Lemkau [274], whilst possibly accepting this position has definite reservations about the assumptions made about the cathartic function of sports. He writes: 'I am a little sceptical, I must admit, about whether athletics are really an outlet for aggressive feelings. It seems to me that the controls involved in game rules are so complete that there is some doubt whether this basic aggression would be released in such a controlled situation. I would at least say that it is a release for the drive to physical activity which is certainly not the same as aggression.'

The danger of hostile acts being committed in competitive forms of physical education can be largely overcome with firm control though hostile feelings may not be able to be fully released within the inhibitory framework of the rules that govern them.

Inherent in individual competition is the possibility that one may become self-interested, vain and motivated only by acts that will lead to self-advantage or self-aggrandisement. Individual competitive sports, of course, have their place in physical education and in many ways they can be socially advantageous [275], but, as Gates [276] has pointed out, there is the danger that, by thinking too much of themselves, individuals sometimes forget to think about others and as a result become indifferent to them. If there is suggestion of this as is the case occasionally with people like athletes, boxers and swimmers, the physical educationist should do his best to get them to join with others from time to time in order that they may share in their social and co-operative undertakings.

A more severe indictment of competition lies in the fact that it frequently involves selection. This means that some are picked and others are not. For those rejected there is the chance that they may feel inferior, resentful or humiliated. Worse, in some ways, especially if they have been dropped from team membership, is the feeling that their social 'in group' status has been undermined. Feelings of this sort cannot ever be entirely overcome where there are a large number of candidates competing for a limited number of places. Some people would question whether it is morally right that some children should have to vie with others. There is some ground for argument here, but there is a difference between children wanting to compete and their being made to compete. It seems reasonable to say that children should not be forced into compulsory representative competition nor should they be sheltered from the known facts of their inequality. On this latter point Reid [277] has this to say: 'It is not the competition or the acknowledgment of inequality as such which is bad, but the making of these inequalities into a main standard of human assessment'. Children need sympathy, yet at the same time they should be brought up resilient enough to be able to overcome the disappointments and upsets that life in its passage will inevitably bring them.

Competition in itself is neither good nor bad, but from it, according to the manner in which it is handled, can stem beneficial or detrimental effects. Some attempt must therefore be made to give a general appraisal of competition and the way it should be conducted.

Summary and Conclusions
The bulk of opinion about the use of organised competition before adolescence is that it should be discriminately and sparingly used. The Joint Committee on Athletic Competition for Elementary and Junior High School age. [278] (a body which comprised psychiatrists, psychologists and experts in child growth and development), felt that 'high pressure' competition was undesirable, and likely to result in a distorted sense of values. It also pointed out that if competition was to be carried on without incurring possible damage there should be no blame attached to 'failure' for it was recognised that although some children take it in their stride and are stimulated by it, some others react to it with feelings of inferiority. Reichert [279], in writing about competitive sport before the 'teens', has drawn attention to the dangers of placing children under the care of parents and teachers who put too much stress

upon winning. Whilst making the observation that competition is an inherent characteristic of 'growing and developing', he recommends amongst other things that: (1) opponents should be matched according to their physical and emotional level as well as to their size, age, bodily build and level of maturity; (2) interschool and intercommunity contests are not to be encouraged for children at this age; (3) intramural competition should be designed to have educational value as well as recreational value.

For boys and girls who never make school teams intramural competition has its advantages. It gives an added spur to effort and the experience of being opposed by different groups, but it should not be over exploited as an administrative convenience for there must be time left for progressive skill practices, appreciation of strategy, and so on. Its chief value should be in extent rather than amount. In this respect house and form matches have their place in most schools. Group strength and group co-operation are best revealed by as many members taking part as is practicably possible.

The health implications connected with competition in physical education are many and varied. In attempting to make a summary of these the following points can be made. They are largely based upon a list originally drawn up by Layman [280]:

1. It can broaden the social horizons of the participant and help to give him an understanding of the fact that individuals in other schools, neighbourhoods, and socioeconomic groups have interests and feelings similar to his. In doing this they help to promote the development of interests in others, understanding of others, and sympathy for others.

2. It can help team members to learn about co-operation and group loyalty, and sometimes these are stronger than the competitive spirit. Often the existence of teams helps to develop a sense of loyalty and in working co-operatively for the group. This can occur even in individuals who are not in the team but who think of the team as 'our team'.

3. It can act as a powerful incentive to learning, especially for those who feel they have a chance of winning. For those who are always losers, however, it may be a deterrent to learning.

4. Particularly for those competing for places in a team, it can lead to the development of hostile feelings for one another. This can be corrected by the teacher if proper emphasis is placed on concepts such as sportsmanship, fairness and friendliness. However, with young children, excessive competition may interfere with the social aspect of character development.

5. Unless special provision is made in the case of a minority, it can lead to emotional disturbance and perhaps, in consequence, to a troubled development of the whole personality.

6. Unless adequate provision is made for extensive intramural competition, it can lead to a few only having the opportunity of testing themselves and deriving the experience of contest.

7. It can lead to beneficial emotio-social effects. These can best be induced, Layman says, when (a) the programme involves varied activities; (b) when it is such that participation is available to all; (c) when approval is given for co-operation, sportsmanship, observing the rules, and trying hard; (d) when joy in the activity is stressed and the importance of winning is not overemphasised; (e) when competition is not surrounded by community hysteria and the loser need not fear blame or rejection when he makes a mistake; and (f) when it is under competent professional leadership.

Throughout this section it has been acknowledged that competition exists in our culture and that its effects in physical education, where it is an inherent part of many of its activities, can be co-operative and advantageous both to the individual and the group or they can be detrimental to the individual and disruptive to the group. The role of the teacher in promoting the advantageous course rather than the disadvantageous course, as in so many other educational undertakings, is crucial. The good teacher can make the advantages of competition, of which we may count co-operation one, very much outweigh its disadvantages. In games it is impossible to do without the element of competition because it is a fundamental part of their nature. If physical educationists cannot be idealists and say with Reid [281] that 'if the use of competition is to be justified,

at some stage it must lead to its own annihilation', t
perhaps join with him when he says that, 'if competiti\
used as a motive . . . it should move to its own subor(
and be lost sight of in concern for things which are worth doing
and enjoying for themselves'.

THE IMPORTANCE AND FUNCTION OF
THE PHYSICAL EDUCATION TEACHER

Frequent reference has been made to the importance of the
teacher in the various fields under discussion. This has been
incidental to our main theme of showing how the activities
with which physical education is concerned contribute to the
development of the personality and to the educative process.
However an integral part of physical education is the role of
the person dealing with it. The personal influence of the
physical educationist can prove to be of tremendous importance.
Not only does he control the physical education programme
which, as we have seen, has so much to offer and all that this
involves in the way of selection and suitability and so on, but
over and above this, and partly because of it, he has unusual
and distinctive opportunities for assisting the young in their
struggle towards adjustment and maturity. This is no less true
in the realm of social development than any other. The
Educational Policies Commission [282] recognised this when it
said that 'because of the close personal relationship between
pupil and teacher, the teacher of sports is usually one of the
most influential members of the school community in the
shaping of moral and spiritual values'. The physical educationist's influence is not only acknowledged by an official
educational body but is upheld by the opinion of the children
themselves. Witty's study [283], showed that boys particularly
displayed much more responsiveness to the teacher who showed
an interest in games and sports. Thus, because of the material
the physical educationist deals with and because of his interest
in it, he has potentially more influence upon the shaping of the
child's personality than most of his colleagues. If one of his aims
is to integrate the individual initiative with an appreciation of
social cohesion and sensitivity, he should go about his task

methodically and with an awareness of his function as a teacher and as a person.

Knowledge of Pupils as an Aid to Teaching
For the well being of the child, the teacher should not only take cognizance of him as a unitary and functioning organism, but try to take stock of his potentialities and needs and work out ways by which they can be catered for and met. This can only be accomplished by assembling information of various kinds and by putting it to use. When the child is at play, for example, the teacher can learn a great deal by alert and perceptive observation. He can see whether or not the child is socially accepted or rejected; or whether he is emotionally secure or insecure. If he is to be efficient he should know as much as he can about the nature of the children so that he can successfully promote their learning. Factors like intelligence, family background, interests and so on are as pertinent to his task as are the factors of somatotype, strength and skill. Assimilated knowledge is never a waste if it can later be applied in the vital act of teaching. A firm grasp of the needs of individual children can often curb the temptation of the teacher to arrange the programme around his own interests and enthusiasms.

In physical education, as in other areas of education, tests and measurements have their use. Information resulting from them can prove to be of value to the teacher in guiding social development. Skubic [284], for example, has shown that knowledge gained by the use of sociometric techniques can be used to good effect in assisting the isolate to interact more freely with those about him. Arnold [285], too, in gaining knowledge about the physical abilities of boys through the use of a battery of tests, found that he was better able to meet their physical and socio-emotional needs by the provision of more homogeneous groupings. Hawcroft [286], amongst others, has spoken of the sociogram as a means by which the teacher can gain knowledge of human relationships in physical education so that he can turn it to good account in the formation of socially compatible groups. This latter point though must be accepted with some reservations. It is one thing to bear them sympathetically in mind but quite another to sacrifice everything to their establishment. As Edwards [287] has pointed out, there are other factors in physical education groupings that must be taken into account if teaching and learning is to proceed efficiently as well as amicably.

Useful though knowledge is in the shape of information and test results, it is only of real use if it is applied wisely and with discretion. Take the case of the use of the sociogram. Anderson [*288*] has this to say: 'Sociograms are of practical value in working with children's groups as they clearly point out isolated and overlooked children who need attention. But there is some question about their contribution to science. . . . Moreover, there is always some question about the generalisations that can be drawn, since they are relative to the particular group on which they are obtained.' The warning here is plain. The physical educationist in his quest for information and statistical findings should not let the limited worth of his results outweigh his overall common sense. The isolate of one situation, for example, basketball, is not necessarily the isolate of another situation, for example, swimming. Before the physical educationist can think about assisting the apparent social deficiency he should first of all see if it generally applies. Before attempting to improve a pupil's standing with his peers by artificial means, such as preferential attention by authority figures, which Reger [*289*] has shown to have negligible success, he should aim to improve the skills which may be preventing him from participating in the group's activities. Similarly the fact that somebody is an isolate does not necessarily mean that he is maladjusted. It could mean that he is the only one who is 'right' in a 'wrong' group. Sociograms unfortunately have their limitations; they present relationships, as Anderson has observed, only in the context of a particular group of people whether their values are good, bad or indifferent. The physical educationist should be aware of the limitations as well as the advantages of the various measuring techniques at his disposal if he is to practise his craft intelligently. The statement by Wall [*290*] that 'a child can only truly be said to be maladjusted when he is unable, to a noticeable and incapacitating extent, to enter freely into the life of his group and to meet the demands it makes upon him in a way which the group itself finds acceptable', should be reviewed with some reservation. Character development, within the definition of this book, is not necessarily the perfect correlate of social adjustment. In cases of grave disparity the educationist and the psychiatrist must agree to part company. Their work, although they have much in common, is different in application. The one is primarily concerned with things as they 'ought' to be the other is primarily concerned with adjustment to things as they 'are'. The one is essentially to do with moral values the other is essentially to do with therapeutic practice. There is no absolute line of demarcation of course on either side. The teacher frequently finds himself attempting to deal with both matters. Dewey [291] partially overcomes this problem by providing us with a rough rule-of-thumb solution. He said: 'Learn to act with and for others while you learn to think and to judge for yourself'. The point about this digression is that measurement is only a part of knowledge and because of this it should be used only with understanding and circumspection. It should be used by the teacher as paint is in the hands of an artist—used, but only when it is pertinent and when it is in keeping with what he is trying to achieve.

It is not that the use of sociograms and sociometry has ever been in question, but rather that there is a danger of it being misused. Sometimes sociometricians, in their zealousness to do good, mistake the trees for the wood and in consequence overstate the worth of their own findings. Nobody would deny that, with or without the aid of sociometry, the physical educationist has 'unique opportunities to study boys and girls as interactive social beings' [292] and that because of this he can often help them either directly or indirectly with their problems.

Attributes of Successful Leaders

Because of his age, specialist training and authoritative position, the professional physical educationist is a leader whether he likes it or not. But because he has authority it does not follow that he has to be dominative. In fact, in a community where democratic living is to be encouraged, it is best that he should not be. He should instead attempt to live out the qualities he is trying to foster. As Williams [293] has succinctly said: 'he who would teach social values must himself first possess them'. The sort of qualities that it is hoped the teacher might possess are the same as those we listed when discussing character. This does not mean that he will be a failure unless he possesses all these qualities. Rather it means that he should be aware of them as ideals and be alive to the idea of embodying them and presenting them whenever he can. Mere possession of desirable traits, however, as recent studies [294] have shown, does not necessarily bring about leadership. A more dynamic and positive approach is required for this.

In speaking of the social development of the young child Isaacs [295] says: 'The educator . . . cannot do her work well unless she attracts to herself mainly the forces of love. . . . She must behave in such a way that the child can love her, even though she uses the love solely for the child's governing and training; she must represent to the child the world of love and creation, and not become associated with that of hatred and destruction.' Good teachers like good parents should become aware of this. They should be active and engaging, affectionate and warm hearted. That qualities like these are appreciated by children is substantiated by the experimental findings of Jennings [296]. She found that leadership was often ascribed to people who gave others 'psychological comfort' and had the ability to make them feel secure, belonged, wanted and of some importance. Witty [297], too, in another study, presents a similar picture. On analysing 12,000 descriptive letters from children and adolescents concerning 'the teacher who helped me the most', he found that attributes which tended to bolster the security and self-esteem of the pupils were valued highly. More specifically speaking, they indicated that, qualities and practices like giving praise and recognition, showing kindliness and fairness, having a sense of humour and an interest in pupil's problems, and being tolerant, sympathetic and considerate were associated with desirable leadership. These are bound up with meeting the individual emotional and social needs of the pupil. All in all, as Leeds [298] has shown, the personality characteristics of the teacher have an effect upon the emotional and social development of the children in his care. If he is to be of help to them he should realise that he must be sensitive towards their difficulties and aware of them as distinct and separate persons.

Psychological Influences and the Role of the Teacher as a Model
It is commonly agreed that the influence of the parents on the growing child is enormous. This comes about by the satisfaction or otherwise of basic needs and by the exposure of the child to the social environment of the home. Among the processes at

work that come to bear upon the child are those of identification, suggestion and imitation. These processes are not the prerogative of the parents; other people, not least of all the physical educationist, use them for good or bad as the case may be. It is known, for example, through such studies as those conducted by Jersild [299] and Symonds [300] that children of school age often tend to identify themselves with a popular teacher (though not necessarily a good one) and not only take on some of his characteristics but actually change some of their behaviour patterns to please him. 'The psychological forces that impel the child to emulate a model' [301] are not necessarily in agreement with what is desirable. However, according to Stoke [302], they are related to the extent to which the child's needs are satisfied. This ties up with what has gone before: that the good teacher is not only the one that possesses good character traits but the one who in addition can meet the emotio-social needs of the child. Because such factors as strength and physical skills are important to the child and to the adolescent in their social dealings the physical educationist has a great opportunity to help them to adjust and to assume 'good' behaviour patterns as opposed to 'bad' by being the sort of person he would like them to be. It is of passing interest to note that another study by Symonds [303] suggests that children who have been taught by teachers who are warm, friendly and encouraging tend to be better adjusted than those who have been taught by teachers who are cold, aloof and critical.

The persuasive power of suggestion is well known to the advertising experts whether done subliminally or at conscious level. The teacher should perhaps be more aware of this same power within himself. By suggestion 'we mean the process of communicating an idea from one individual to another, when the idea is accepted more or less uncritically or without rational ground' [304]. In the activities of physical education, where the teacher's personality is often seen to be in action, the teacher should be careful to present a good example himself if he wants certain ideals and standards to be adopted by others. If he wants fairness on the rugby field, for example, he should be an exemplar of fairness himself. Still more he should see that fairness is done and, if possible, let it be seen that fairness is done. As a model and as a guide his role is important. Apart from the question of example other factors can help determine the effectiveness of suggestion. Two of these, to use Lumley's terms [305], are repetition and volume. The first is concerned with frequency and implies that the teacher should never be content with just saying or doing something once if he wants the point assimilated. The second is concerned with intensity. This implies that spectacular and deeply experienced events can have sudden and marked effects. Both factors, it will be observed, are in keeping with the laws of learning. The physical educationist should be aware of the susceptibility of children to the processes of identification and suggestion. It is only by a lively awareness of their power that he will remember (assuming he is not perfect in all respects!) to present a good and consistent pattern of behaviour that will implant itself in the minds and habits of his pupils.

Complementing the processes of identification and suggestion is the process of imitation. Its place in the child's social behaviour has been strikingly illustrated by Miller and Dollard [306]. Although the term has been used in several different ways* the use which is most commonly adopted is the one which relates to 'performing an act seen performed by another' [307]. It is a characteristic of play and in adolescence it often manifests itself in an act of hero-worship. Cooley [308] writes of this latter phenomenon as follows: 'It has a great place in all active aspiring lives, especially in the plastic period of youth. We feed our characters, while they are forming upon the vision of admired models; an ardent sympathy dwells upon the traits through which their personality is communicated to us—facial expression, voice, significant movements and so on. In this way those tendencies in us that are toward them are literally fed; are stimulated, organised, made habitual and familiar.'

The physical educationist has a big responsibility here. It is well known that because he (or she) is concerned with, and often good at, games he becomes the subject of hero-worship. There is nothing wrong with this so long as the model presented is worthy of imitation. It is particularly likely to occur, as Cooley observes, at an impressionable and susceptible phase in growing up and it is therefore important that a desirable person should be fulfilling the role of model. Since some degree of imitation is almost inevitable it is incumbent upon the physical

* See Decroly O. *Comment l'enfant arrive à parler*, Vols. I and II. Cathiers de la Centrale. Cent du P.E.S. de Belgique, Vol. 8, 1934.

educationist to present himself not only as a person to be admired for his skill, but for his qualities of good character as well.

It appears also that not only matters of conduct are affected by imitation. Bandura and Walters [309], for example, have shown, in an experiment that centred on a bowling game, that the adult model was imitated with regard to his standards and his level of aspiration by the children with whom he was playing. His influence in connection with these matters, it is of interest to note, were retained by the children even when left to continue playing on their own. Clearly the role of the teacher as a model has many repercussions beyond those that are immediately apparent. Because of this it is highly desirable that the physical educationist should not only appear to be, but actually be a person of the highest calibre both in and outside his sphere of work.

Self-knowledge and Individual Guidance

Because physical education teachers tend to be of predominantly mesomorphic build they must try to be sensitive to the needs of those who are not, both at a physical and temperamental level. This involves an understanding and knowledge of the pupils with whom the physical educationist is concerned and an understanding and knowledge of himself. If he does not sometimes try to look at himself objectively he may find himself puzzled at his unusual appreciation of one pupil's problems on the one hand and an inability to appreciate the problems of a second pupil on the other. Unless he tries to develop some self-knowledge he may find himself reacting 'to an extent he seldom suspects in terms of his own needs and his own personality problems'. He may tend 'to feel close to those pupils whose interests or problems parallel his own'. Of these processes:

> The teacher may be totally unaware, recognising only his likes and dislikes easily rationalising them as sound personality evaluations. He may find hostile adolescent behaviour particularly hard to face; he may be repelled beyond reason by over-dependent pupils or he may be tempted to let them lean upon him too heavily; he may need the affection of his pupils too much, or be unable to accept it at all . . .
>
> Personal reactions of this sort cannot be entirely avoided; they are part and parcel of every human being. But the more consciously

such aspects in a situation can be recognised, the less they tend to distort relations, and to hamper critical judgement. . . .

The real point for our purposes is that the teacher:

> Needs to understand not only his students' problems but his own as well and be aware of the fact that he too is at any instant operating in a total situation, a situation which among other things includes his own history and personality. It needs no further elaboration to point out that such self-awareness is an essential equipment of all who choose work with children as their primary task. [310]

If self-knowledge is a desirable aim of the physical educationist so too is his awareness and sympathy for others. In the group situations with which he is so frequently confronted he must never lose sight of an individual's requirements. He must be quick to see the opportunities that present themselves to bring about the continued growth of the individual boy or girl. As Dewey [311] says: 'On one side it is his business to be on the alert to see what attitudes and habitual tendencies are being created. In this direction he must, if he is an educator, be able to judge what attitudes are conducive to continued growth and what are detrimental.' He must be sure enough and perceptive enough to see whether or not a child needs individual guidance. It is likely that the child who shows no respect for the property of others, or who is loud-mouthed and vulgar needs to be taken on one side and talked to about rectifying these and similar deficiencies. All problems cannot be overcome by personal counselling, however, and it may be necessary at times to send a hypersensitive or hydrophobic child, for example, to somebody who is more competent to deal with him. A great deal, nevertheless, can be accomplished by the physical educationist in shaping the character and personality of his pupils on a face to face basis and he should never through laziness or other controllable weaknesses shirk from his responsibility to do so. In his handling of children and situations too, the physical educationist should not find himself working to prescribed or previously-found-to-be-successful formulas. He may find that what is apparently the same is in fact different. As Buber [312] has remarked: 'In spite of all similarities, every living situation has, like a newborn child, a new face that has never been before and will never come again. It demands of you a reaction which cannot be prepared beforehand. It demands nothing of what is past. It demands presence, responsibility; it demands you.' To the teacher of physical education this direct and personal advocacy of the teacher/pupil relationship is particularly gratifying. He alone among the staff of a school actually handles the child in helping him to overcome some of his fears and challenges. In touching the legs, arm, back or stomach of a child a unique bond is set up. Through bodily contact, however slight, and the bringing of a new achievement with which it is often accompanied, the physical educationist can set alight in the child the flames of new confidence and a new understanding. As Meredith [313] has observed, achievement for the child is bound up with what he can do with his body. If he associates his own welfare and progress with the contact, help and sympathy he gets from the teacher, as he often does, he may look to him for assistance in the future, not only in the physical and perhaps obvious sense, but in the psychological sense too. This dependence and faith of the young child in the physical educationist, with his strong, secure and reassuring arms, can often be of immense comfort and strength to him in the tasks and skills with which he is confronted. Both in the gymnasium and in the swimming bath it is possible to see the most improbable achievements come about as a result (to a great extent at any rate) of the implicit trust of the child in the teacher. This is not without its dangers. On the one hand the child needs the help of the teacher but on the other hand too much dependence is not good for him. He must at some point learn to become self-confident and self-reliant. The responsibility of the physical educationist lies in seeing how and when the transition should take place. This, of course, will vary from one individual to another. As Buber says, each situation has a new face.

The shaping of character and personality is not always bound up with such subtle complexities either. In the straightforward bestowal of reward and punishment, or praise and criticism, the physical educationist can often do effective work. In the bestowal of praise, for example, he should try to be discriminate and make allowance for individual differences. He should give it only to those who have deserved it by a good deed or a worthy achievement. It should not be dolloped out like so many spoonfuls of sugar in recognition of token levels of accomplishment. Poor performers should be equally eligible if they do something that is praiseworthy by *their* standards. In short, praise should be earned rather than awarded. It should, if possible, have the emotional accompaniment of satisfaction too, if it is to be used as a form of motivation to repeat the same act or to produce others in a similar vein [*314*]. In the same way, and in keeping with the laws of learning, punishment, in the shape of a rebuke for dishonesty, for example, can often dissuade the offender from doing the same thing again. Although this in itself may not meet all the implications of good moral teaching it does fulfil the purpose of indicating that it is not a characteristic of behaviour that is acceptable to the teacher or to the pupil's fellows if they are, as they may be in a game, adversely affected by it. This last point leads on to a consideration of the role of the physical educationist in relation to the group.

Group Membership and Leadership

Because the physical educationist, like his colleagues, is an adult and in a position of authority, he can never be fully accepted as a member of the pupil-groups with whom he works. However, unlike many of his colleagues, he can often participate in their games and in their recreative pursuits. This camaraderie, often involving common aspirations, common victories and common defeats, enables him to exercise an influence over the group's affairs and to an extent help its individual members. The participatory effect of the teacher on younger children is particularly noticeable. Its value is clearly illustrated by Hartley, Frank and Goldenson [*315*], for instance, when they write of the teacher of music and movement. 'If she merely stands by and directs,' they say, 'the children tend to feel estranged, isolated and at loose ends. But when she is hopping, skipping, tumbling, or acting like a gust of wind or a rabbit, the situation is structured so that a feeling of "we-ness" predominates. She can play a cherishing role for those who need "mothering" and are too shy to ask for it. . . . As long as she remains within the group, she also offers support for those who are not yet ready to sustain continuous contact on their own.'

With older children this in-group membership is often more difficult to attain, but again the physical educationist has an advantage over the majority of his colleagues in that many of the activities with which physical education is to do predispose themselves to group effort and this sometimes enables him to enter into it by contributing something towards its objectives and aims. If he can offer what the group wants, then there is a good chance of his assuming the actual leadership on the 'inside' rather than having a nominal leadership from the 'outside'. As Zeleny [316] has said: 'Leadership is . . . a phase of social process in which the most adaptable and useful members emerge as representing the values most desired by the group at that time'. Not only this, he goes on to say: 'A leader is the centre of the social potential of the group'. If this is true it is clear that the physical educationist should be in a position to wield a fair amount of influence for good. He has an opportunity to direct the thoughts and actions of group members to those qualities we mentioned in discussing the nature of character. This, however, is not easy. He may first have to assume the group's values. In order to make secure the position of leadership, to quote Zeleny again, he may have to 'share the values held by the group, and then, being ambitious and persistent, use his knowledge, intelligence, vitality, self-confidence and social adaptability to become the most active and acceptable member; in other words, the leader's talents must be used in vital participation in group activity and in re-directing group activity to satisfy human needs'. He need not stop at this point either. The meeting of human needs is one thing; the influencing of thought, values and conduct is another. As a group leader he should aim to do both. He must aim to guide and direct the group in such a way that he is able to influence it to do as *he* wants and yet, at the same time, give its members the feeling that they are doing what *they* want. As a professional leader he should be able to turn a knowledge of group dynamics to good account.

It is perhaps reassuring to our democratic way of life that in an experiment carried out by Lippitt and White [317] on groups of 10-year-old boys to do with their reaction to three varieties of adult leadership (authoritarian, democratic, laissez-faire) it was to leadership of the democratic kind that they responded best. In the democratic 'atmosphere' group problems were discussed by all group members. The democratic leader participated in this but only in a 'factual' or 'objective' way before the group made its final decisions. In comparison with both other forms of leadership, where decisions were either dictated or not entered into at all, the democratic climate produced a great deal less irritability and aggression. In comparison with the authoritarian climate it was as much as thirty times less marked. The experiment appears conclusive enough in its implications for social education but the children upon whom it was carried out were American and therefore brought up in a democratic climate. This may account in part at least for the big difference in hostility between the democratic climate and the authoritarian. Even so there is an important lesson here for teachers in democratic communities. It is that if one wants social harmony and group-decision-making, a good leader, in the form of the teacher, is necessary. He can help the group by originating ideas and by co-ordinating the ideas of others in the direction of common group purposes. He can act in a way that calls forth initiative, resourcefulness and enthusiasm from each and every member of the group. Teaching and learning in the social field in our society should result in a co-operative enterprise in which the teacher should play the part of an enlightened and democratic leader. In this process the physical educationist because of the unusual circumstances that surround his work can offer a great deal.

BOOKS FOR FURTHER READING

Bandura, A. and Walters, R. H., *Social Learning and Personality Development*. Holt, Rinehart and Winston, 1963.

Breckenridge, M. E. and Vincent, E. L., *Child Development*. W. B. Saunders, 1960.

Buber, M., *Between Man and Man*. Boston. Beacon Press, 1955.

Castle, E. B., *Moral Education in Christian Times*. George Allen and Unwin, 1958.

Coleman, J. S., *The Adolescent Society*. N.Y. Free Press of Glencoe, 1961.

Denney, R., 'American Youth Today' in E. H. Erikson's *Youth: change and challenge*. Basic Books, 1963.

Fleming, C. M., *Adolescence: It's Social Psychology*. Routledge and Kegan Paul, 1948.

Foss, B. M., 'Imitation' in *Determinants of Infant Behaviour*. Methuen, 1966.

Hartley, R. E., Frank, L. K. and Goldenson, R. M., *Understanding Children's Play*. N.Y. Columbia University Press, 1952.

Isaacs, S., *Social Development in Young Children*. Routledge, 1943.

James, J. M., *Education and Physical Education*. Bell, 1967.

Jersild, A. T., *Child Psychology*. N.Y. Prentice Hall, 1947.

Jones, H. E., *Motor Performance and Growth*. Berkeley University of California Press, 1949.

Lehman, H. C. and Witty, P. A., *The Psychology of Play Activities*. N.Y. Barnes, 1927.

McIntosh, P. C., *Sport and Society*. C. A. Watts and Co., 1963.

Nahapiet, K. H., 'The Contribution of Physical Education to the Development of the Personality' in *Physical Education Association Yearbook*, 1964–5.

Peck, R. F. and Havighurst, R. J., *The Psychology of Character Development*. Wiley, 1960.

Piaget, J., *The Moral Judgement of the Child*. London. Kegan Paul, 1932.

Reid, L. S., *Philosophy and Education*. Heinemann, 1962.

Russell, Bertrand A. W., *History of Western Philosophy*. Allen and Unwin, 2nd Edn., 1962.

Sapora, A. V. and Mitchell, E. D., *The Theory of Play*. Ronald, 1961.

Sherif, M. and Sherif, C. W., *An Outline of Social Psychology*. Harper and Row, 1956.

—— *Groups in Harmony and Tension*. N.Y. Harper, 1953.

Williams, J. F., *The Principles of Physical Education*. W. B. Saunders Co., 1964.

CHAPTER SIX

PHYSICAL EDUCATION AND THE NEEDS OF SOCIETY

PHYSICAL EDUCATION AND THE NEEDS OF SOCIETY

Society today with its problems of mass media, mental sickness and affluence which were discussed in the opening chapter, has three main needs of physical education. These may be termed educational, psycho-social and bio-philosophic.

Educational Need
According to Dewey's principle of 'continuity of experience' education should be a process of growth which, in theory at least, should be lifelong. With few people can this be said to occur. For the great majority the educative process almost stops dead from the moment they leave school and as a result many of them suffer from an indulgent apathy which is marked by passivity and a loss of identity.

The results of the extension of popular education has in few instances led to the continuous enrichment of the personality as at one time it had been hoped. Hoggart [*318*], for example, in surveying the effects that a newly acquired literacy has had on the habits and attitudes of today's working-class urban communities, presents a sorry and vapid picture. Instead of the gains in awareness and appreciation one would expect, the ordinary person neither has the wish nor the ability to go on learning for himself. He is no longer personally active and prefers to sit, passively absorbing the banal notions of mass media. This lack of self-activity and lack of interest in things other than the materialistic leads to a gradual impoverishment of the personality which is characterised in many people today by a moral turpitude and a lack of individuality. The sociologist has noticed that modern society, with its hidden persuaders [*319*] that insinuate towards conformity, tends to sweep the individual into a pool of social and spiritual vacuity. This state of 'other directedness', as Riesman [*320*] calls it, is becoming increasingly common and something must be done to stop its malignancy before it infects the whole of society. There may be some comfort in the increase in leisure hours that automation can bring about; man will have an opportunity as never before to continue with his own development. Yet he must be helped and guided if boredom is not to destroy this new-found freedom and render it a burden.

If in the age of leisure—and it is reckoned [321] that by the year A.D. 2000 over one quarter of the average person's life-span will be spent on pursuits of his own choosing—man is to use his time profitably (and in accord with Dewey's concept of growth) he must be kept active. In this engagement of man physical education has an important contribution to make. About this Riesman [322] makes the following comment:

> The first step may consist of giving play a far higher priority as a produce both of society and character than we give it today . . . play, from having to be the residue sphere left over from work time and work feeling, can increasingly become the sphere for the development of skill and competence in the art of living. Play may prove to be the sphere in which there is still room for the would-be autonomous man to reclaim his individual character from the pervasive demands of his social character.

Indeed physical education as part and parcel of continuative and recreative education has a great many things to offer. It is essentially a personal and direct form of educational experience and through its skills, joys, satisfactions, discoveries and achievements a great deal can be done to enliven and enrich the life of man.

In the chivalrous code of sportsmanship there is also much that is of educational value. In Webster's dictionary sportsmanship is defined as 'conduct becoming to a sportsman, involving honest rivalry and graceful acceptance of results'. In a fiercely competitive world it is of social significance to have standards that call upon a sense of fairness and a consideration for the other man. Its intrinsic co-operativeness brings a fellowship to its exponent's affairs without a loss of identity. Cozens and Stumpf [323] think so highly of it that they speak of it in the following panegyrical terms: '. . . in a world that has no common religious or political philosophy to share, perhaps the field of sport and the universality of the ideal of sportsmanship may provide a meeting ground where co-operation and understanding, a respect for the rules, and a sense of fair play will prevail'.

Another value of physical education is that it is active and *re*-creative. As we have noted it gathers experience at first hand and by so doing gives opportunity for spontaneity and self-expression which can sometimes be accompanied by a heightened perception and awareness of one's 'self'. In some forms of dance, for example, where room is left for extemporisation and fluidity of movement, such opportunities will come naturally and through them an acquired aggregate of self-knowledge will develop. This is all part of the individuation process with which education is partially concerned. By a variety of unique and varied experiences the danger of uniformity can, to some extent, be avoided. Lest it should be thought, however, that the state of self-realisation is incompatible with sociability it must be remembered that self-realisation, as Storr [324] points out, is a fulfilment of the total personality of which the social aspect is a part. Indeed the welfare of society as a whole is furthered through attention to self- or individual education.

Psycho-social Need
The second need society has of physical education is the psycho-social one. Halliday [325] coined the phrase 'sick society' because of the amount of ill-health (particularly mental), that there is in our community. By way of remedy he offers the term 'integrated health' which is virtually synonymous in meaning with the psychiatric concept of 'integrated personality'. Different expressions such as these reinforce the idea that man reacts to his environment as a whole. His functions and aspects of personality cannot be compartmentalised if his health and well-being are to be preserved. In touching upon the meaning of health we are once more reminded of our fundamental hypothesis of balance.

It is known that both in the United States [326] and in England and Wales [327] over half of the hospital beds are filled with mental patients. Mental illness in fact is as prevalen as all other forms of illness put together [328]. In a society in which improved methods of sanitation and nutrition have greatly reduced positive physical sickness we are left contrariwise with an increased amount of disturbance which takes its origin in our psycho-social life. To what causes can these less easily explained forms of illness be attributed? They seem to lie largely in the imbalance of modern life with its intensity, loneliness, monotony and commuter travel. The social strain of status seeking, too, must take its toll [329]. Whatever the reasons, the prominence of mental illness in the industrialised West is in sharp contrast to the more natural and integrated life of primitive peoples. Margaret Mead [330], for example, in studying the Samoan peoples, records that mental disease was an extremely rare phenomenon. Whilst it would be wrong and in any case quite impossible to abdicate from our more civilised state, something ought to be done to rectify the imbalance that has arisen.

A child can gain release and integration through imaginative play [331]. It is not unreasonable to suppose that something along the same lines might be possible for the adult through recreational play [332]. There is some evidence to support this view. Menninger [333] said, writing as a clinical psychiatrist: 'Good mental health is directly related to the capacity and the willingness of an individual to play. Regardless of his objections, resistances, or past practice, any individual will make a wise investment for himself if he does plan time for his play and take it seriously.' The psychological rule of attention upholds the view that if concentration on one thing is replaced by concentration on another, relief is gained from the first piece of concentration. It seems to follow from this, that if, after work, man can turn to play for relaxation he is likely to gain relief from the tensions and pressures that pre-occupation with one aspect of his life can give. However, it is not just relief that is wanted (that can be achieved by the recumbent watching of television) but an active and educative outlet. Physical education is well qualified to cater for this dual requirement. Whilst the Greeks looked to the theatre for *katharsis* we can look to physical activity for the same purpose. Through the manifold nature of its activities physical education can do much to alleviate the frustrations, anxieties, pressures and strains that the pattern of modern society imposes. Urges, impulses and aggressions can to some extent, at least, be sublimated into a beneficial and acceptable framework of behaviour. The avoidance of loneliness and the need for acceptance can both be satisfied through the co-operative participation that is a feature of many of physical education's activities. The face-to-face relationship that is a part of many games and sports can bring a better understanding of one's fellow men and in the sharing of a common objective a basic satisfaction. Physical education, in fact, may be regarded not only as an antidote to the stresses of modern living [334] but as a form of therapeutic and preventive medicine which takes its place alongside innumerable other measures that contribute to the all-embracing concept of health.

We may get a better picture of the sort of person we are looking for by quoting what Vincent [335] considers to be the characteristics of a healthy personality:

> The healthy personality . . . has vitality, courage, and interest; is alert, decisive, prompt, direct, objective, resourceful, neat though not a slave to neatness, honest though not rude, humble though self-respectful, confident but not arrogant; it is kind, tolerant, reverent, is moderate in appetites. It has a sane attitude toward religion, toward marriage and toward authority. It appreciates its own strength and its own weaknesses; it has a sense of proportion, a sense of humour, a love of beauty, and a love of its fellow men.

Physical education can help considerably in bringing on many of these qualities and by doing so can do considerable service to society.

Bio-philosophic Need

'The Affluent Society', as Galbraith has dubbed ours [336], has many features which can be associated with physical enfeeblement. The ease and softness of life no longer make demands on the human organism that test and strengthen. The numerous labour-saving devices may be regarded almost as commensurate with body-weakening. The promise of a still further extension of the use of automation in the produce of goods is likely to reduce the necessity for physical powers still more. This growing obsolescence in the necessity for physical fitness and hardiness in our day-to-day living, which has accelerated considerably in the past twenty years, is in the long run debilitating to man's constitution. This has not gone altogether unnoticed. Alexander [337], for example, writing as early as 1910 said: 'The truth is that man, whether living in town or country, has changed his habitat, and with it his habits, and in doing so has involved 'himself in a new danger, for though evolution may be cruel in its methods, it is the cruelty of a discipline without which our bodies become relaxed, our muscles atrophied, and our functions put out of gear'.

It would be comforting to think that the detrimental effects of inefficient body functioning—the area with which Alexander was largely concerned—has improved in recent years but what evidence there is is disappointing. Writing almost half a century later Mitchell and Mason [338], after examining a number of researches conducted in the 1930s, made this comment: 'It seems safe to assume from these statistics that at the time the studies were made not more than 25% of our youth possessed good body mechanics, and there is no reason to believe the situation is materially better today'.

Although it is quite true that positive signs of organic ill-health have declined in the last fifty years, since the coming of increased medical knowledge and a growing social consciousness for the welfare of people, the general capacity for efficien and prolonged manual labour, has undoubtedly diminished. What average office worker for instance could stand up to the physical strain of working on a farm? This of course, is not saying that he still hasn't the inherent ability—he has. It is rather that the ease with which life can be lived has sapped man of his vitality and energy.

Perhaps the most notable philosophic expression of man's progressive biological degeneracy is found in Spengler's [339] *Decline of the West*. In talking of man's slavish dependency on the machine he was revealing what seemed to him a justifiable despair of industrialised man's future. Fortunately the pessimism that was current in the 1920s and 1930s under the influence of Spengler's depressing prognostications was dissipated in the cataclysmic events of the Second World War. Since then the new evolutionary biology of men like Huxley [340], Medawar [341] and Waddington [342] gives a much needed reassurance that man can, if he will, help in the control of his own destiny. This lies in the ability of man to transmit ideas. One of the new ideas that has been transmitted in the last few generations is a way of thinking based on scientific method. It is the hope of the future that man may apply some scientific thinking to bring about the biological rejuvenation of himself. This obviously cannot be accomplished by a regression to primitivism but it can be by a vigorous reassertion of its importance in a philosophic and practical framework. Already man has sensed the need for a re-examination of the place in life of his own biological constitution. Alexander's pioneering attempts [343] to rehabilitate man's physical inadequacies by what he called 'conscious control' has been supplanted by more modern approaches of which we may count the science of ergonomics one. Easily the most significant contribution, however, in re-establishing the importance of man's essentially biological nature is found in the bio-social philosophy of Dewey. In its approach to education it takes note of man's learning propensities by recognising that experience comes to man partly through the biological properties he has at his command. The activity of which he speaks refers not only to the mental but to the physical aspects of man. Whilst some aspects of Dewey's theory of education may be criticised the fundamental acceptance of them is axiomatic to our future—at least until replaced by a philosophy that is similarly directed.

Even in Dewey, however, the body is seen primarily as an instrument through which it is possible to learn rather than as a unit which must be kept fit. The two are not mutually exclusive. It will be seen that ability to learn with the aid of the physical ultimately depends upon the state of the organism. If its powers are declining, the ability to learn some things will be proportionately reduced. Basic physiological qualities like strength and endurance matter, and so too do the mental correlates like discipline, concentration and perseverance. This lack of attention to the long-term inheritance of man is a weakness in Dewey. He capitalises on the fact that he has a body but omits to suggest how this side of man's future can be best assured.

It was William James [344] who, writing in the growing shadows of the First World War, first sensed the need for the maintenance of physical and mental resilience in times of peace when he spoke of 'the moral equivalent of war'. Although an advocate of peace he recognised that the militarist concerns of hardihood and discipline were of value if society was to remain vigorous and manly. He, therefore, suggested an army that would enlist against Nature so that such qualities that have been mentioned could be wrought into the growing fibre of the people. A concrete exposition of what he had in mind in order to retain the virility and vitality of man lies in these words:

> To coal and iron mines, to freight trains, to fishing fleets in December, to dish-washing, clothes-washing, and window-washing, to road-building and tunnel making, to foundries and stokeholes and to the frames of skyscrapers, would our gilded youth be drafted off, according to their choice, to get the childishness knocked out of them, and to come back into society with healthier sympathies and soberer ideas. They would have paid their blood-tax, done their own part in the immemorial human warfare against nature; they would tread the earth more proudly, the women would value them more highly, they would be better fathers and teachers of the following generation.

The practical application of a vision such as this would be difficult and probably in any case prove unacceptable in a democratic society that is as proud of personal liberty as ours is. That such a spirit should be kept alive, however, is essential if the dignity of man is to be upheld. In the absence of a way of life that will in a natural manner look after the physical and moral needs of society we must turn instead to the artificed work of the physical educationist. It is to him we largely entrust 'Man's Supreme Inheritance'.

BOOKS FOR FURTHER READING

Bagrit, L., *The Age of Automation*. Penguin, 1965.
Brightbill, C. K., *Man and Leisure*. Prentice Hall, 1961.
Cowell, C. C., *Scientific Foundation of Physical Education*. Harper, 1953.
Galbraith, J. K., *The Affluent Society*. Hamish Hamilton, 1958.
Goldhamer, H. and Marshall, A. W., *Psychosis and Civilisation*. Free Press of Glencoe, 1953.
Hoggart, R., *The Uses of Literacy*. Penguin, 1958.
Huizinga, J., *Homo Ludens: A Study of the Play Element in Culture*. Routledge and Kegan Paul, 1949.
Jokl, E., *Medical Sociology and Cultural Anthropology of Sports and Physical Education*. Thomas, 1964.
Mead, M., *Coming of Age in Samoa*. Penguin, 1961.
Medawar, P. B., *The Future of Man*. Methuen, 1960.
Miller, N. P. and Robinson, D. M., *The Leisure Age*. Wadsworth, 1963.

Packhard, V., *The Hidden Persuaders*. Penguin, 1960.
—— *The Status Seekers*. Penguin, 1959.
Paterson, A. and Hallberg, E. C., *Background Readings for Physical Education*. Winston, 1965.
Riesman, D., *Abundance for What*. Chatto and Windus, 1964.
—— *Individualism Reconsidered*. Free Press, 1965.
Stafford-Clark, D., *Psychiatry Today*. Penguin, 1961.
Selye, H., *The Stress of Life*. McGraw-Hill, 1956.
Spengler, O., *The Decline of the West*, Allen and Unwin, 1938.
Storr, A., *The Integrity of the Personality*. Penguin, 1960.
Tibble, J. W., 'Physical Education and the Educative Process', *Studies in Education*. London Univ. Inst. of Education, 1952.

LIST OF REFERENCES

1. Eysenck, H. J., *The Structure of Human Personality*. Methuen, 1960, p. 2.
2. Pythagoras—Pythagorian Quartet, see *The Greek Experience*, C. M. Bowra. Weidenfeld and Nicolson, 1957, p. 86.
3. Plato. *Republic*, translated F. M. Cornford. Clarendon Press, Oxford, 1941.
4. Jacks, L. P., *The Education of the Whole Man*. U.L.P., 1931.
5. Jeffreys, M. V. C., *Personal Values in the Modern World*. Penguin, 1962.
6. Schweitzer, Albert, *Civilisation and Ethics*. Unwin, 1961.
7. Dewey, J., *Experience and Education*. Macmillan, N.Y., 1946.
   —— *Democracy and Education*. Macmillan, N.Y., 1916.
8. Pinion, F. B., *Educational Values in an Age of Technology*. Maxwell, 1964.
9. Brameld, T. B. H., *Toward a Reconstructed Philosophy of Education*. Dryden, N.Y., 1956.
10. *Ibid*. See Ref. 5 above.
11. Durkheim, E., *Suicide*. Routledge and Kegan Paul, 1952.
12. Riesman, D., *The Lonely Crowd*. Yale University Press, 1950.
13. Halliday, J. L., *Psycho-social Medicine: A Study of the Sick Society*. Heinemann, 1949.
14. Carstairs, G. M., *This Island Now*. Penguin, 1964, p. 21.
15. Fromm, E., *The Fear of Freedom*. Kegan Paul, French Trubner and Co., 1942.
16. Jung, C. G., *Psychology and Religion*. Routledge and Kegan Paul, 1958.
17. *The Crowther Report*, '15 to 18'. H.M.S.O., 1959, p. 171.
18. *Ibid*. See Ref. 3, p. 88.
19. *Ibid*. See Ref. 6, p. 236.
20. Mumford, L., *The Condition of Man*. Martin Secker and Warburg, 1944, p. 416.
21. Gesell, A. L., *Infant Development: the Embryology of Early Human Behaviour*. Harper, N.Y., 1952.
22. Goldstein, K., *Organism: a Holistic Approach to Biology*. American Book Co., N.Y., 1939.
23. Thomson, J. A., *Towards Health*. Putnam, 1927, pp. 3–4.
24. Mohr, R., 'Die wechselwirkung korplicher und seelischer fakteren im krankheitgeschen', *Klin. Wschr.*, 1927. No. 6, pp. 772–6.

25. Brouha, L., 'Training' an article in *Science and Medicine of Exercise and Sports*, ed. by W. R. Johnson. Harper, N.Y., 1960.

26. Jones, H. E., 'The Development of Physical Abilities', *Yearb. Nat. Soc. Stud. Educ.*, 1944. No. 43, pp. 100–22.

27. Witty, P. A., 'A Study of One Hundred Gifted Children', *Univ. Kan. Bull. Educ.*, State T.C. Stud. Educ., Part I. No. 13, 1930.

28. Terman, L. M. and Oden, M., *The Gifted Child Grows Up*. Stanford Univ. Press, 1947.

29. Page, C. G., 'Case Studies of College Men with Low Physical Fitness Indices'. Master's Thesis, Syracuse Univ., 1940.

30. Coefield, J. R. and McCollum, R. H., 'A case study Report of 78 University Freshmen with Low Physical Fitness Indices.' Microcarded Master's Thesis, Univ. Oregon, 1955.

31. Garrison, K. C., *Growth and Development*. Longmans, 1960, p. 463.

32. Asher, R. A. J., 'The dangers of going to bed', *Brit. Med. J.*, 1947. No. 2, pp. 967–8.

33. Abramson, A. S., 'Atrophy of Disuse', *Arch. Phys. Med.*, 1948. No. 29, pp. 562–70.

34. *Ibid*. See Ref. 25, p. 405.

35. Mellerowicz, H. v., quotation taken from an article by J. B. Wolffe, 'Prevention of Disease through Exercise and Health Education', in *Health and Fitness in the Modern World*. Athletic Institute, 1961.

36. Gesell, A., from an article on 'The Ontogenesis of Infant Behaviour' in *Manual of Child Psychology*, ed. L. Carmichael, 2nd edition Wiley, N.Y., 1954, p. 358.

37. Dennis, W., 'The effect of restricted practice upon the reaching, sitting and standing of two infants', *J. Genet. Psychol*. No. 47, pp. 17–32. 1935.

38. Hilgard, E. R., *Introduction to Psychology*. Methuen, 1962, p. 70.

39. McGraw, M. B., *Growth: A Study of Johnny and Jimmy*. Appleton-Century, N.Y., 1935.

40. *Ibid*. See Ref. 36.

41. Piaget, J., *The Origin of Intelligence in the Child*. Routledge and Kegan Paul, 1935, p. 357.

42. Hebb, D. O., *A Textbook of Psychology*. Saunders, 1958.

43. Gesell, A. and Ames, L. B., 'The Ontogenetic organisation of prone behaviour in human infancy', *J. genet. Psychol*. No. 56, pp. 247–63. 1940.

44. Lewin, K., 'Behaviour and Development as a Function of the Total Situation', in *Handbook of Child Psychology*. See Ref. 36.

45. Ribble, M. A., *The Rights of Infants: early psychological needs and their satisfaction.* Columbia Univ. Press, N.Y., 1943.
46. Gesell, A. L., (i) *The First Five Years of Life.* Harper, N.Y., 1940. and Ilg, F., (ii) *The Child from Five to Ten.* Harper, N.Y., 1946.
47. Wetzel, N. C., *Wetzel Grid: a technique for evaluating Physical Fitness in terms of growth and development.* Dept. of Nat. Health and Welfare, Ottawa, 1940.
48. Wear, C. L. and Miller, K., 'Relationship of Physique and Developmental level to Physical Performance', *Res. Quart.*, Dec., 1962.
49. Adams, E. H. A., 'A comparative anthropometric study of hard labour during youth as a stimulator of physical growth of young coloured women', *Res. Quart.*, 1938. No. 9, pp. 102–8.
50. (i) Van Dusen, C. R., 'An anthropometric study of the upper extremities of children', *Human Biol.*, 1939. No. 11, pp. 277–84.
    (ii) Buskirk, E. R., Anderson, K. L. and Brozek, J., 'Unilateral activity and bone and muscle development in the forearm', *Res. Quart.*, 1956. No. 27, pp. 127–31.
51. *Ibid.* See Ref. 36.
52. Bayley, N., 'The development of motor abilities during the first two years', *Soc. Res. in Child Devt. Monogr.*, 1936, No. 1.
53. Shirley, M. M., *The First Two Years.* Univ. of Minnesota Press, Minneapolis, 1933.
54. McGraw, M. B., 'Maturation of Behaviour', in *A Manual of Child Psychology*, ed. L. Carmichael. Wiley, N.Y., 1946.
55. Stoddard, G. D. and Wellman, B. L., *Child Psychology.* Macmillan, N.Y., 1934.
56. Gutteridge, M. V. A., 'A Study of Motor Achievements of Young Children', *Arch. Psychol.*, 1939, p. 244.
57. *Ibid.* See Ref. 38, pp. 71–3.
58. Jones, T. D., 'The development of certain motor skills and play activities in young children', *Child Devt. Monogr.*, No. 26, 1939.
59. Isaacs, S., *The Nursery Years.* Routledge and Kegan Paul, 1932.
60. Munrow, D., *Pure and Applied Gymnastics.* Arnold, 1957.
61. Ministry of Education, *Moving and Growing.* H.M.S.O., London, 1952.
62. Randall, M. W. and Waine, W. K., *Objectives of the Physical Education Lesson.* Bell and Sons, 1955, p. 145.
63. *Ibid.* See Ref. 60 above.

64. Jones, H. E., 'The development of physical abilities in adolescence', *National Year Book for the Study of Education*, Part I, 1944.

65. Jones, H. E., *Motor Performance and Growth. A developmental study of dynamometric strength*. Univ. Calif. Press, Berkeley, 1949, p. 181.

66. Meredith, H. V., 'The rhythm of Physical Growth: a study of 18 anthropometric measurements on Iowa City males range in age between birth and 18 years', *Univ. of Iowa Stud. in Child Welfare*, 1935, No. 11, p. 3.

67. Tanner, J. M., *Growth at Adolescence*. Blackwell, 1962, p. 203.

68. Espenschade, A., 'Motor Performance in Adolescence' in R. G. Kuhlen and G. G. Thompson's, *Psychological Studies of Human Development*. Appleton-Century-Crofts, N.Y., 1952.

69. Goodenough, F. L., 'The development of the reactive process from early childhood to maturity', *Journal of Experimental Psychology*, 1935, Vol. 18, pp. 431–50.

70. Philip, B. R., 'Reaction time of Children', *Amer. J. of Psychol.*, 1934, Vol. 46, pp. 379–96.

71 Wild, M. R., 'The behaviour pattern of throwing and some observations concerning its course of development in children', *Res. Quart.*, Oct. 1938, pp. 20–4.

72. Brace, D. K., *Measuring Motor Ability*. Barnes, N.Y., 1927.

73. Dimock, H. S., 'Research in Adolescence. 1. Pubescence and Physical Growth', *Child. Devt.*, 1935. No. 6, pp. 177–95.

74. Espenchade, A., 'Motor Development' in *Science and Medicine of Exercise and Sports*, W. R. Johnson. Harper, N.Y., 1960. pp. 430–1.

75. Heath, S. R., 'The rail walking test: preliminary maturational norms for boys and girls', *Motor Skills Res. Exchg.*, 1949, No. 1, pp. 34–6.

76. Hupprich, F. L., 'A study of flexibility of girls in five age groups'. Doctor's dissertation, Univ. of Oregon, 1949.

77. Jokl, E. and Cluver, E. H., 'Physical Fitness', *Journal of the American Medical Association*, 1941, Vol. 116, pp. 2, 382–3, 389.

78. *Ibid.* See Ref. 74 above.

79. Kretschmer, E., *Physique and Character*. Springer, Berlin, 1948.

80. Sheldon, W. H.:
   (i) *The Varieties of Human Physique*. Harper, N.Y., 1940.
   (ii) *The Varieties of Temperament*. Harper, N.Y., 1942.
   (iii) *Atlas of Men*. Harper, N.Y., 1954.

81. Eysenck, H. J., *The Structure of the Personality*. Methuen, 1953.

82. Hall, G. S. and Lindsay, G., *Theories of Personality*. Wiley, 1957, p. 374.
83. (i) Cureton, T. K., *Physical Fitness appraisal and guidance*. Mosby, St. Louis, 1947.
    (ii) Lindegard, B., *Body build, body-function and personality*. Lund: C. W. K. Gleerup, 1956.
    (iii) Sills, F. D. and Everett, P. W., 'The relationship of extreme somatotypes to performance in motor and strength tests', *Res. Quart.*, 1953, No. 24, pp. 223–8.
84. Cureton, T. K., *Physical Fitness of Champion Athletes*. Univ. of Illinois Press, Urbana, 1951.
85. Tanner, J. M., *The Physique of the Olympic Athlete*. Allen and Unwin, 1964.
86. Arnold, P. J.:
    (i) 'The Need for Selection', *Physical Education*, Nov., 1960.
    (ii) 'Somatotype, Physical Ability and Intelligence', *The Leaflet*, May, 1962, pp. 28–9.
87. *Ibid*. See Ref. 67, p. 98.
88. Parnell, R. W., *Behaviour and Physique*. Arnold, 1958.
89. Carter, J. E. L.,
    (i) 'The Physiques of Male Physical Education Teachers in Training', *Physical Education*, Nov., 1964.
    (ii) 'The Physiques of Female Physical Education Teachers in Training', *Physical Education*, March, 1965.
90. *Ibid*. See Ref. 88, p. 58.
91. Vernon, P. E., *Intelligence and Attainment Tests*. U.L.P., 1960, p. 158.
92. Hebb, D. O., *The Organisation of Behaviour*. Wiley, N.Y., 1948, pp. 294–6.
93. Ribble, M. A., *The Rights of Infants*. Columbia Univ. Press, N.Y., 1943, p. 9.
94. Bowlby, J., *Child Care and the Growth of Love*. Penguin, 1961, p. 47.
95. *Ibid*. See Ref. 94, p. 19.
96 Andry, R. G., *Delinquency and Parental Pathology*. Methuen, 1960, pp. 127–8.
97. Bradley, J., 'Educational and Social Failure: some further observations', *Nature*, Vol. 204, No. 4954, pp. 132–4.
98. *Ibid*. See Ref. 92.
99. Bexton, W. H., Heron, W. and Scott, T. H., 'Effects of Decreased Variation in the Sensory Environment', *Canad. J. Psychol.*, 1954, No. 8, pp. 70–6. Quotation taken from Hebb, 'The Mammal and His Environment', in *Readings*

in Social Psychology by E. E. Maccoby, T. M. Newcomb and E. L. Hartley, Methuen, 1959.

100. Schaffer, H. R., 'Objective Observations of Personality Development in Early Infancy', *Brit. J. Med. Psychol.*, 1958, No. 31, p. 174.
101. *Ibid.* See Ref. 99. Article appertaining to D. O. Hebb, p. 337.
102. Guilford, J. P., 'The Structure of Intellect', *Psychol. Bull.*, No. 53, pp. 267–93.
103. Piaget, J., *The Origin of Intelligence in the Child*. Routledge and Kegan Paul, 1953.
104. Wall, W. D., *Education and Mental Health*. U.N.E.S.C.O. Printed by I.F.M.P.R., Paris, 1964, p. 65.
105. Mellor, E., *Education through Experience in the Infant School Years*. Blackwell, 1953.
106. Pestalozzi, *The Swansong*, 1826. See *Pestalozzi's Educational Writings*, J. A. Green, p. 290.
107. Piaget, J. See Ref. 103. Also:
    (i) *The Psychology of Intelligence*. Routledge and Kegan Paul, 1950.
    (ii) *The Language and Thought of the Child*. Harcourt, Brace, N.Y., 1926.
    (iii) *Judgment and Reasoning in the Child*. Harcourt, Brace, N.Y., 1928.
    (iv) *Play, Dreams and Imitation in Childhood*. Heinemann, 1951.
108. Thurstone, L. L., 'Primary Mental Abilities', *Psychometr. Monogr.* No. 1. Univ. of Chicago Press, 1938, pp. 434, 449.
109. Dewey, J., *How We Think*. Heath and Co., Boston, 1933, p. 89.
110. Watson, J. B., *Behaviourism*. Norton, N.Y., 1930, pp. 267–8.
111. McCarthy, D., 'Language Development in Children' in *Manual of Child Psychology*, ed. L. Carmichael. 2nd edition. Wiley, N.Y., 1954, pp. 587–8.
112. Miller, N. E. and Dollard, J., *Social learning and Imitation*. Yale Univ. Press, 1941.
113. Munn, N. L., 'Learning in Children' in *Manual of Child Psychology*, ed. L. Carmichael. 2nd edition 1954, p. 397.
114. Kulcinski, L., 'Relation of intelligence to the learning of fundamental muscular skills', *Res. Quart.*, Vol. 16, 1945, pp. 266–76.
115. *Ibid.* See Ref. 86.
116. Oliver, J. N. See Ref. 117, p. 92.
117. Knapp, B., *Skill in Sport*. Routledge and Kegan Paul, 1963, p. 92.
118. Burnett, I. and Pear, T. H., 'Motives in Acquiring Skill', *B.J.P.*, Vol. 16, Part 2, 1925, pp. 77–85.

119. Jacks, L. P., *Education Through Recreation*. U.L.P., 1932, p. 39.

120. *Ibid*. See Ref. 60, p. 229.

121. (i) Thorndike, R. L., 'Constancy of the I.Q.', *Psychol. Bull.* 1940, No. 37, pp. 167–86.
     (ii) Knapp, B. See Chapter 2 of Ref. 117.

122. Stroud, J. B., 'The Role of Practice in Learning' in 41*st Yearbook of the National Society for the Study of Education*, ed. N. B. Henry. Univ. of Chicago Press, 1942.

123. Knapp, C. G. and Dixon, W. R., 'Learning to Juggle'.
     (*a*) *Res. Quart.* Vol. 21, 1950, pp. 331–6.
     (*b*) *Res. Quart.* Vol. 29, 1958, pp. 32–6.

124. Cozens, F. W., 'A comparative Study of two methods of teaching classwork in track and field events', *Res. Quart.* Vol. 2, pp. 75–9.

125. Scott, M. G., 'Learning rate of beginning swimmers', *Res. Quart.* Vol. 25, 1954, pp. 91–9.

126. Bell, H. M., 'Rest pauses in motor learning as related to Snoddy's hypothesis of mental growth', *Psychol. Monogr.* 1942, 54. No. 1.

127. Travis, R. C., 'The effect of the length of the rest period on motor learning', *J. Psychol.*, 1937, No. 3, pp. 189–94.

128. Bartlett, F. C., *Psychology and the Soldier*. Camb. Univ. Press, 1927.

129. *Ibid*. See Ref. 117, p. 54.

130. Johnson, G. B., 'Motor Learning' in W. R. Johnson's *Science and Exercise of Medicine and Sports*. Harper, N.Y., 1960.

131. Hilgard, E. R., *Introduction to Psychology*. Methuen, 1957, pp. 261–3.

132. Cross, T. J., 'A comparison of the whole method, the minor game method and the whole-part method of teaching basketball to ninth grade boys', *Res. Quart.* Vol. 8, No. 4, 1937, pp. 49–54.

133. Niemeyer, R. K., 'Part versus whole methods and massed versus distributed practice in the learning of selected large muscle activities'. Graduate dissertations, Univ. of S. Carolina, June, 1958.

134. Rodgers, E. G., 'An experimental investigation of the teaching of team games', *Contributions to Education*, No. 680. Teachers College, Columbia Univ., N.Y., 1936.

135. Priebe, R. E. and Burton, W. H., as reported by Meer, A. W. V. in 'The economy of time in industrial training. An experimental study of the use of sound films in the training of lathe operators', *J. Ed. P.* Vol. 36, 1945, pp. 65–90.

136. Lockhart, A., 'The value of the motion picture as an instructional device in learning a motor skill', *Res. Quart.* Vol. 15, 1944, pp. 181–7.

137. Brown, H. S. and Messersmith, L., 'An experiment in teaching tumbling with and without motion pictures', *Res. Quart.* Vol. 19, 1948, pp. 304–7.

138. Kinnear, A. D., 'Making Swimming a Pleasure', *Sport and Recreation.* Vol. 1, No. 4, 1960, pp. 14–17.

139. Goodenough, F. L. and Brian, C. R., 'Certain factors underlying the acquisition of motor skill by pre-school children', *J. Exp. P.* Vol. 12, 1929, pp. 127–55.

140. Metheny, E. and Ellfeldt, L., 'Dynamics of Human Performance', in *Health and Fitness of the Modern World.* Athletic Institute, U.S.A., 1961, pp. 282–9.

141. *Ibid.* See Ref. 124.

142. Clarke, L. V., 'Effect of Mental Practice on the development of a certain skill', *Res. Quart.* Vol. 31, 1960, pp. 560–9.

143. *Ibid.* See Ref. 131, pp. 263–5.

144. See Woodworth, R. S. and Schlosberg, H., *Experimental Psychology.* Chapter on Transfer and Interference. Holt, N.Y., 1954.

145. Munn, N. L., 'Bilateral transfer of training', *J. Exp. P.* Vol. 15, 1932, pp. 343–53.

146. Bartlett, F. C., *The Mind at Work and Play.* Allen and Unwin, 1951, p. 141.

147. *Ibid.* See Ref. 117, p. 105.

148. Judd, C. H., 'The Relation of special training of general intelligence', *Educ. Rev.* No. 36, 1908, pp. 28–42.

149. Hendrikson, G. and Schroeder, W. H., 'Transfer of Training in learning to hit a submerged target', *J. Educ. Psychol.* Vol. 32, 1941, pp. 205–13.

150. Mohr, D. R. and Barrett, M. E., 'Effect of knowledge of mechanical principles in learning to perform intermediate swimming skills', *Res. Quart.* Vol. 33, No. 4, Dec., 1962.

151. McCloy, C. H., 'The Mechanical Analysis of Motor Skills' in *Science and Medicine of Exercise and Sports*, W. R. Johnson. Harper, N.Y., 1960, pp. 54–64.

152. Dyson, G. H. G., *The Mechanics of Athletics.* U.L.P., 1962.

153. Whitehead, A. N., *Science and the Modern World.* C.U.P., 1927.

154. Cowell, C. C., *Scientific Foundations of Physical Education.* Harper, N.Y., 1953, p. 222.

155. Witty, P., 'An analysis of the Personality Traits of the Effective Teacher', *J. of Ed. Research*, May, 1947, pp. 662–71.

156. Dewey, J., *Experience and Education*. Macmillan, N.Y., 1938, p. 51.
157. *Ibid*. See Ref. 154, p. 103.
158. Bowlby, J., *Maternal Care and Mental Health*. W.H.O., Geneva, 1952.
159. Freud, S. See *A Primer of Freudian Psychology* by Hall, C. S. Mentor Book, 1960, pp. 102–12.
160. Jersild, A. T., 'Emotional Development' in *Manual of Child Psychology*, ed. L. Carmichael. 2nd edition, Wiley, 1954, p. 833.
161. Gesell, A., *Youth: the years from Ten to Sixteen*. Hamish Hamilton, 1956, p. 329.
162. Bridges, K. M. B., 'Emotional Development in Early Infancy', *Child Developm*. No. 3, 1932, pp. 324–34.
163. Symonds, P. M., *The Dynamics of Human Adjustment*. Appleton-Century-Crofts, N.Y., 1946.
164. Jersild, A. T. and Holmes, F. D., *Children's Fears*. Teachers College, Columbia University, N.Y., 1935.
165. Cannon, W. B., *The Wisdom of the Body*. Kegan, Paul, Trench, Trubner and Co. 2nd edition, 1947.
166. Young, P. T., *Motivation and Emotion*. Wiley, 1961, pp. 454–6.
167. Rennie, T. and Woodward, L., *Mental Health in Modern Society*. The Commonwealth Fund, 1948, p. 333.
168. *Ibid*. See Ref. 104, p. 236.
169. White, R. W., *The Abnormal Personality: a textbook*. Ronald, N.Y., 1948.
170. Meredith, G. P., 'Personal Education' in *P.E.A. Year Book*. 1964-5, p. 41.
171. Macmurray, J., *Reason and Emotion*. Faber and Faber, 1935, p. 44.
172. *Ibid*. See Ref. 160, p. 854.
173. Murray, V., quote taken from *The Education of the Emotions* by M. Phillips. Allen and Unwin, 1937, p. 14.
174. Axline, V. A., *Play Therapy*. Houghton Mifflin, 1947, p. 9.
175. Thomas, W. I., *The Unadjusted Girl*. Little Brown, Boston, 1923.
176. Bowley, A. H., *The Natural Development of the Child*. E. & S. Livingstone, 1957, p. 58.
177. *Ibid*. See Ref. 174, p. 16.
178. (a) Isaacs, S., *Intellectual Growth in Young Children*. Routledge, 1930, p. 102.
     (b) Klein, M., *The Psychoanalysis of Childhood*. Hogarth Press, 1932, p. 246.
179. Freud, S., *Beyond the Pleasure Principle*. Int. Psychoanalytical Press, 1922, p. 15.
180. *Ibid*. See Ref. 46 (No. ii), p. 286.

181. Hadfield, J., *Psychology and Morals: an analysis of Character.* Methuen, 1939.

182. *Ibid.* See Ref. 174.

183. Jackson, L. and Todd, K. M., *Child Treatment and the Therapy of Play.* Methuen, 1948.

184. *Ibid.* See Ref. 154.

185. Mill, J. S., *Utilitarianism, Liberty and Representative Government.* Dent, 1948, p. 117.

186. Hall, G. Stanley, *Adolescence: its psychology and its relations to physiology, anthropology, sociology, sex, crime, religion and education.* 2 Vols. Appleton, N.Y., 1904, p. 214.

187. Laban, R., *Modern Educational Dance.* MacDonald and Evans, 1948, p. 11.

188. Ellis, Havelock, *The Dance of Life.* Houghton Mifflin, 1923, p. 60.

189. *Ibid.* See Ref. 186, p. 60.

190. Maslow, A. H., 'Self Actualising People. A study of psychological health', *Personality Symposia.* No. 1, p. 16. See also *Current Concepts of Positive Mental Health* by M. Jahoda. Basic Books, N.Y., 1958, p. 71.

191. Reid, L. A., *Philosophy and Education.* Heinemann, 1962, pp. 63 and 100.

192. Nunn, P., *Education: its Data and First Principles.* Arnold, 3rd edition, 1960, p. 185.

193. Bender, L. and Boas, F., 'Creative dance in Therapy', *Amer. J. Orthopsychiat.,* 1941. No. 11, pp. 235–44.

194. Chace, M., 'Dance as an adjunctive therapy with hospitalised mental patients', *Bull.,* Menninger Clin., 1953. No. 17, pp. 219–25.

195. May, R., 'Modern Dancing as a therapy for the mentally ill', *Occup. Ther. and Rehabilit.* 1941. No. 20, pp. 101–7.

196. Rosen, E., 'Dance as a therapy for the mentally ill', *Teach. Coll. Rec.* 1954. No. 55, pp. 215–22.

197. Layman, E. M., 'Contributions of Exercise and Sports to Mental Health and Social Adjustment' in *Science and Medicine of Exercise and Sports,* W. R. Johnson. Harper, N.Y., 1960.

198. Jersild, A. T. and Holmes, F. D., *Children's Fear.* Teachers College, Columbia Univ., N.Y., 1935.

199. McCloy, H. C., *Philosophical Bases of Physical Education.* Appleton-Century-Crofts, 1940, p. 14.

200. Adler, A., *Study of organ inferiority and its physical compensation.* Nervous and Mental Disease Publishing Co., N.Y., 1917.

201. *Ibid.* See Ref. 46 (i), p. 356.

202. Jeans, P. C., 'Feeding of healthy infants and children', *Journal of the American Medical Association*, 1950, Vol. 142, Pt. 2, p. 810.
203. Cowell, C. C., 'The Contributions of Physical Activity to Social Development', *Res. Quart.*, May 1960.
204. Bridges, K. M. B., *Social and Emotional Development of the Pre-School Child*. Kegan Paul, London, 1931.
205. Isaacs, S., *Social Development in Young Children*. Routledge, 1933, p. 394.
206. Levy, D. M., *Maternal Overprotection*. Columbia Univ. Press, N.Y., 1943.
207. *Ibid.* See Ref. 205, p. 428.
208. *Ibid.* See Ref. 105, p. 155.
209. Hartley, R. E., Frank, L. K. and Goldenson, R. M., *Understanding Children's Play*. Columbia Univ. Press, N.Y., 1952, pp. 313 and 370.
210. McKinney, F., *Psychology of Personal Adjustment*. Wiley, N.Y., 1949, pp. 413–15.
211. Cowell, C. C., 'An abstract of a study of differentials in junior high school boys based on observation of physical education activities', *Res. Quart.*, 6, 1935, pp. 129–36.
212. Reuter, E. B., Foster, R. G. and Mead, M., *et al*, 'Sociological research in adolescence', *Americ. J. Sociol.*, 42, pp. 81–94, 1936.
213. Sollenberger, R. T.
    (i) 'The Concept of Adolescence', *Psychol. Bull.*, 36, p. 601, 1939.
    (ii) 'Some relationships between the urinary excretion of male hormone by maturing boys and their expressed interests', *J. Psycho.*, 9, pp. 179–89, 1940.
214. Nahapiet, K. H., 'The Contribution of Physical Education to the Development of the Personality'. Article in *Phy. Edn. Assn. Year Book*, 1964–5, p. 16.
215. Lehman, H. C. and Witty, P. A., *The Psychology of Play Activities*. Barnes, N.Y., 1927.
    See also Witty, P. A., 'A Study of Deviates in Versatility and Sociability of Play Interest', *Teach. Coll. Contrib. Educ.*, 1931, No. 470.
216. Cowell, C. C., 'Student Purposes in High School Physical Education', *Edn. Res. Bull.* (Ohio State Univ.), 18, pp. 89–92, April, 1939.
217. Foehrenbach, L. M., 'Why Girls Choose After-School Sports', *Journal of American Assn. for Health, Physical Education, Recreation*, 24, pp. 34–8, June, 1953.

218. *Ibid.* See Ref. 26, pp. 101 and 117.
219. Biddulph, L. G., 'Athletic achievement and the personal and social adjustment of high school boys', *Res. Quart.*, 25, 1954, pp. 1–7.
220. Oliver, J. N., 'The Relationship between Physical Characteristics and The Social and Emotional Characteristics of Educationally Sub-Normal Boys', *Wing* No. 2, June, 1964.
221. Jones, H. E., *Motor Performance and Growth.* Univ. of Calif. Press, Berkeley, 1949, p. 167.
222. Jones, H. E., 'Physical Ability as a Factor in Social Adjustment in Adolescence', *J. educ. Res.*, 1946, 40, p. 297.
223. Oliver, J. N.:
   (i) *Ibid.* See Ref. 220.
   (ii) 'The effect of physical conditioning exercises and activities on the mental characteristics of educationally sub-normal boys', *Brit. J. Educ. Psycho.*, 28, pp. 155–65.
  Kane, J. E.:
   'The Relationship between Physical and Social Characteristics', *Wing* No. 2, pp. 15–24, June, 1964.
224. *Ibid.* See Ref. 221.
225. Arnold, M., *Culture and Anarchy: an essay in political and social criticism.* Murray, 1920.
226. McIntosh, P. C., *Sport and Society.* C. A. Watts and Co. Ltd., 1963.
227. Denney, R., 'American Youth Today', contribution in E. H. Erikson's *Youth: change and challenge.* Basic Books, 1963, pp. 131–51 (p. 138).
228. Horrocks, J. E., *The Psychology of Adolescence.* Houghton Mifflin, Boston, 1951, pp. 258–60.
229. Brace, D. K., 'Sociometric Evidence of the Relationship Between Social Status and Athletic Ability among Junior High School Boys', *Professional Contributions*, No. 3. American Academy of Physical Education, Washington, D.C., 1954.
230. Coleman, J. S., *The Adolescent Society.* Free Press of Glencoe, N.Y., 1961, p. 147.
231. Murphy, L. B., *et al, Experimental Social Psychology.* Harper, N.Y., 1937.
232. Jones, V., 'Character Development in Children—an objective approach'. Article in L. Carmichael's *Manual of Child Psychology.* 2nd Edition, Wiley, 1954, p. 783.
233. (i) Russell, Bertrand, A. W., *History of Western Philosophy and its connection with political and social circumstances from*

earliest times to the present day. Allen and Unwin, 2nd edn., 8th impression, 1962.

(ii) Castle, E. B., *Moral Education in Christian Times.* Allen and Unwin, 1958.

234. Toulmin, S. E., *The Place of Reason in Ethics.* Cambridge Univ. Press, 1953, p. 170.

235. MacMurray, J., in his Gifford Lectures (1954) called 'The Form of the Personal'. Later published in two volumes:
(i) *The Self as Agent.* Faber, 1957.
(ii) *Persons in Relation.* Faber, 1957.

236. (i) *Ibid.* See Ref. 232.
(ii) *Ibid.* See Ref. 38, pp. 72–8.

237. Piaget, J., *The Moral Judgement of the Child.* Kegan Paul, London, 1932.

238. *Ibid.* See Ref. 46 (ii), pp. 356–8.

239. *Ibid.* See Ref. 232, p. 826.

240. Hartshorne, H. and May, M. A., *Studies in Deceit: Book I, General. Methods and Results: Book II, Statistical. Methods and Results.* Macmillan, N.Y., 1928.

241. Kilpatrick, W. H., *Foundations of Method.* Macmillan, N.Y., 1925, p. 340.

242. Neumann, H., *Education for Moral Growth.* Appleton and Co., N.Y., 1923, p. 191.

243. Thrasher, F. M., *The Gang: a study of 1313 gangs in Chicago.* Univ. of Chicago Press, 1927.

244. Sherif, M. and Sherif, C. W., *An Outline of Social Psychology.* Harper and Row, 1956, pp. 280–332.

245. Jones, V., *Character and citizenship-gaining in the public school.* Univ. of Chicago Press, 1936.

246. (i) Drinkwater, D. J., 'An assessment of the value of physical education in character training for boys', M.A. thesis. University of London, 1956, p. 110.

(ii) Feder, D. D. and Miller, L. W., 'An evaluation of certain aspects of a programme of character education', *Educ. Psychol.* No. 24, 1933, pp. 385–91.

(iii) Rarick, G. L., 'Physical Education' in *Encyclopaedia of Educational Research,* 1960.

(iv) Milverton, F. J., 'An experimental investigation into the effect of physical training on personality', M.A. thesis. Univ. of Leeds, 1940.

(v) Olson, W. C., 'Character Education' in *Encyclopaedia of Educational Research,* ed. W. S. Monroe. 1941, p. 124.

247. Mitchell, E. D. and Mason, B. S., *The Theory of Play.* A. S. Barnes, N.Y., 1948, pp. 288–9.

248. *Ibid.* See Ref. 175.

249. Trevelyan, G. M. Address given at Aberdovey to Outward Bound in 1943. Contained in *Outward Bound*, ed. D. James. Routledge and Kegan Paul, 1957, p. 14.

250. Lunnon, V. M., 'Outward Bound', in *Physical Education*. Vol. 50, No. 150, July, 1958, p. 60.

251. Young, G. W., 'The influence of the mountains upon the development of human intelligence'. Pamphlet. Jackson, Glasgow, 1957.

252. *Ibid.* See Ref. 154, p. 231.

253. Williams, J. F., *The Principles of Physical Education*. 8th edition. W. B. Saunders Co., 1964, p. 155.

254. Mead, M. *et al.*, *Co-operation and competition among primitive peoples*. McGraw Hill, N.Y., 1937.

255. Greenburg, P. J., 'Competition in Children: an experimental study', *Amer. J. Psychol.*, 1932. No. 44, pp. 221–48.

256. Murphy, G., *Personality*. Harper, N.Y., 1947, p. 525.

257. Maller, J. B., 'Co-operation and Competition: an experimental study in motivation', *Col. Univ. Contrib. to Educ.* No. 384, Col. Univ., N.Y., 1929.

258. (i) Leuba, C., 'An experimental study of rivalry in young children', *J. Comp. Psychol.*, 1933, No. 16, pp. 367–78.
    (ii) Wolf, T. H., 'The effect of praise and competition on the persisting behaviour of kindergarten children', *Inst. Child Welf. Monogr.*, 1938. No. 15.
    (iii) Gates, A. I., Jersild, A. T., McConnell, T. R. and Challman, R. C., *Educational Psychology*. Macmillan, N.Y., 1948, pp. 150–2, 286–7.

259. *Ibid.* See Ref. 112.

260. Midcentury White House Conference on Children and Youth, *A Healthy Personality for Every Child*. Health Publications Inst., Raleigh, North Carolina, 1951.

261. Russell, B., *Education and the Modern World*. Norton, N.Y., 1932, p. 237.

262. (i) Hurlock, E. B., 'An evaluation of certain incentives used in school work', *J. educ. Psychol.*, 1925. No. 16, pp. 145–59.
    (ii) *Ibid.* See Ref. 254.
    (iii) *Ibid.* See Ref. 256.

263. Breckenridge, M. E. and Vincent, E. L., *Child Development*. W. B. Saunders, 1960, p. 482.

264. *Ibid.* See Ref. 205, p. 454.

265. Klein, M., *The Psychoanalysis of Children*. Norton, N.Y., 1932, p. 124.

266. Sherif, M. and Sherif, C. W., *Groups in Harmony and Tension*. Harper, N.Y., 1953.

267. Cerf, W., 'Sponsorship of Democracy', *J. High Educ.*, Oct., 1946, pp. 364–8.

268. (i) Johnson, W. R. and Harmon, J. M., 'The emotional reactions of college athletes', *Res. Quart.* 1952. No. 23, pp. 391–7.

  (ii) Johnson, W. R. and Hutton, D. C., 'Effects of a combative sport upon personality dynamics as measured by a projective test', *Res. Quart.* 1955. No. 26, pp. 49–63.

  (iii) Johnson, W. R., 'A study of emotion revealed in two types of athletic sports contests', *Res. Quart.* 1949. No. 20, pp. 72–9.

269. Johnson, W. R., 'Needed Research on the Effects of Physical Education Activities upon Personality'. Paper read at the Coll. Phys. Educ. Assn., Daytona Beach, Dec., 1955, p. 432.

270. *Ibid*. See Ref. 253, p. 77.

271. *Ibid*. See Ref. 104, p. 138.

272. *Ibid*. See Ref. 268 (ii).

273. Kahn, M., 'A polygraph study of the catharsis of aggression'. Unpublished, Harvard Univ., 1961.

274. Lemkau, P. V., *Desirable Athletic Competition for Children*. A.A.H.P.E.R. (N.E.A.), 1952, p. 17.

275. Annarino, A. A., 'The Contribution of Athletics to Sociability'. Unpublished M.A. thesis, Purdue Univ., June, 1951.

276. *Ibid*. See Ref. 258 (iii).

277. Reid, L. S., *Philosophy and Education*. Heinemann, 1962, p. 135.

278. *Ibid*. See Ref. 197, p. 580.

279. Reichert, J. L., 'Competitive Sports before the Teens', *Today's Health*. No. 35. Oct., 1957, pp. 28–31.

280. *Ibid*. See Ref. 197, p. 582.

281. *Ibid*. See Ref. 277.

282. Education Policies Commission, *Moral and Spiritual Values in the Public Schools*. National Education Association, Washington, 1951, p. 68.

283. *Ibid*. See Ref. 155.

284. Skubic, E., 'A Study of Acquaintanceships and Social Status in Physical Education Classes', *Res. Quart.* March, 1949. No. 20, pp. 80–7.

285. *Ibid*. See Ref. 86 (i).

286. Hawcroft, E. G., 'Group Interaction in Physical Education', *Physical Education*. March, 1960, pp. 15–18.

287. Edwards, K. J., 'Group Interaction in Physical Education', *Physical Education*. July, 1960, p. 47.

288. Anderson, J. E., 'Methods of Child Psychology' in *Manual of Child Psycholgy*, ed. L. Carmichael, 2nd edition. Wiley, N.Y., 1954, p. 26.

289. Reger, R., 'An attempt to integrate a group isolate', *Res. Quart*. May, 1962.

290. *Ibid*. See Ref. 104, p. 237.

291. Dewey, J., 'Some aspects of modern education', *School and Society*. 1931. No. 34, pp. 579–84.

292. Cowell, C., 'The Guidance Functions and Possibilities of Physical Education', *The Journal of the American Association for Health, Physical Education and Recreation*. April, 1949, p. 288.

293. *Ibid*. See Ref. 270.

294. (i) Zeleny, L. D., 'Leadership' in *Encyclopaedia of Educational Research*. Macmillan Co., 1950, p. 664.

   (ii) Bavelas, A. and Lewin, K., 'Training in Democratic Leadership', in *J. Abnorm. Soc. Psychol*. 1942. No. 37, pp. 115–19.

295. *Ibid*. See Ref. 205, p. 410.

296. Jennings, H. H., 'Leadership—A Dynamic Re-definition', *Journal of Educational Sociology*. March, 1944, pp. 431–3.

297. *Ibid*. See Ref. 155.

298. Leeds, C. H., 'Teacher Behaviour Liked and Disliked by Pupils', *Education*. Sept., 1954. No. 75, pp. 29–36.

299. Jersild, A. T., *Child Psychology*. Prentice Hall, N.Y., 1947.

300. Symonds, P. M., *The Ego and the Self*. Appleton-Century-Crofts, N.Y., 1951.

301. Bronfenbrenner, U., 'Freudian theories of identification and their derivatives', *Child Devt*. 1960. No. 31, pp. 15–40.

302. Stoke, S. M., 'An inquiry into the concept of identification', *J. Gen. Psychol*. 1950. No. 76, pp. 163–89.

303. Symonds, P. M., *The dynamics of parent-child relationships*. Teachers College, Columbia Univ., N.Y., 1949.

304. Ellwood, C. A., *The Psychology of Human Society*. D. Appleton and Co., N.Y., 1925, p. 347.

305. Lumley, F. E., *Principles of Sociology*. McGraw-Hill, N.Y., 1928, p. 224.

306. *Ibid*. See Ref. 112, pp. 168–81.

307. Drever, J., *A Dictionary of Psychology*. Penguin, 1952, p. 128.

308. Cooley, C. H., *Human Nature and the Social Order*. Charles Scribner, N.Y., 1922, p. 312.

309. Bandura, A. and Walters, R. H., *Social Learning and Personality Development*. Holt, Rinehart and Winston, 1963, p. 179.

310. Blos, P., *The Adolescent Personality*. Appleton-Century-Crofts, N.Y., 1941, pp. 500–1.

311. *Ibid.* See Ref. 7 (ii), p. 33.

312. Buber, M., *Between Man and Man.* Beacon Press, Boston, 1955, p. 114.

313. *Ibid.* See Ref. 170, p. 40.

314. *Ibid.* See Ref. 232, p. 815.

315. *Ibid.* See Ref. 209, p. 337.

316. *Ibid.* See Ref. 294, p. 664.

317. Lippitt, R. and White, R. K., 'An experimental study of leadership and group life' in *Readings in Social Psychology,* ed. T. M. Newcomb and E. L. Hartley. Holt, N.Y., 1952, pp. 315–30.

318. Hoggart, R., *The Uses of Literacy.* Penguin, 1958.

319. Packhard, V., *The Hidden Persuaders.* Penguin, 1960.

320. *Ibid.* See Ref. 12, pp. 318–19.

321. Still, J. W., 'Boredom—The Psycho-Social Disease of Aging', *Gereatrics.* Sept., 1957. No. 12, p. 577.

322. *Ibid.* See Ref. 12, pp. 326–8.

323. Cozens, F. W. and Stumpf, F. S., *Sports in American Life.* University of Chicago Press, 1953.

324. Storr, A., *The Integrity of the Personality.* Penguin, 1960.

325. *Ibid.* See Ref. 13.

326. (i) Moulton (ed.), 'Mental Health—Publication of the American Association for Advancement of Science'. No. 9, p. 211. Science Press, 1939.

(ii) Goldhamer, H. and Marshall, A. W., *Psychosis and Civilisation.* Free Press of Glencoe, 1953.

327. Stafford-Clark, D., *Psychiatry Today.* Penguin, 1961, p. 257.

328. (i) Howard, F. E. and Patry, F. L., *Mental Health.* Harper, N.Y., 1935, p. 486.

(*ii*) *Facts on Mental Health and Mantal Illness.* Public Health Service Publication No. 543, U.S. Govt. Printing Office, 1962.

329. Packhard, V., *The Status Seekers.* Penguin, 1959.

330. Mead, M., *Coming of Age in Samoa.* Penguin, 1961.

331. (i) *Ibid.* See Ref. 174.

(ii) *Ibid.* See Ref. 183.

332. Wessell, J. A. and Huss, W. V., 'Therapeutic Aspects of Exercise in Medicine', in *Science and Medicine of Exercise and Sports,* W. R. Johnson. Harper, 1960, p. 665.

333. Menninger, W. C., 'Recreation and Mental Health', *Recreation.* Nov., 1948. No. 42, pp. 340–6.

334. Selye, H., *The Stress of Life.* McGraw-Hill, 1956.

335. Vincent, L., 'Physical Education's Contribution to the Men~
     Health of Students', *The Journal of Health and Physica~
     Education*. April, 1933.
336. Galbraith, J. K., *The Affluent Society*. Hamish Hamilton, 1958.
337. Alexander, F. M., *Man's Supreme Inheritance*. Methuen, 1918,
     p. 5.
338. *Ibid*. See Ref. 247, p. 197.
339. Spengler, O., *The Decline of the West*. Allen and Unwin, 1938,
     pp. 499–507.
340. Huxley, J. S., *The Humanist Frame*. Allen and Unwin, 1961.
341. Medawar, P. B., *The Future of Man*. Methuen, 1960.
342. Waddington, C. H., *The Nature of Life*. Allen and Unwin, 1960.
343. *Ibid*. See Ref. 337, pp. 168–74.
344. James, William, *Memories and Studies*. 1911. See M. Knight's
     William James. Penguin, 1954, pp. 247–8.

AUTHOR INDEX

Andry, R. G., 51, 74
Annarino, A. A., 117
Arnold, M., 101
Arnold, P. J., 1, 45, 59, 122
Asher, R. A. J., 20
Axline, V. A., 80, 81, 83, 92, 138

Bagrit, L., 142
Bandura, A. and Walters, R. H., 128, 133
Bartlett, F. C., 62, 68, 74
Bavelas, A. and Lewin, K., 125
Bayley, N., 30
Bell, H. M., 62
Beloe Report, 12
Bender, L. and Boas, F., 88
Bernstein, B. B., 56
Bexton, W. H., Heron, W. and Scott, T. H., 52
Biddulph, L. G., 100
Bilodeau, E. A., 74
Blos, P., 129
Bowlby, J., 51, 74, 75
Bowley, A. H., 81, 92
Bowra, C. M., 15
Brace, D. K., 102
Bradley, J., 51
Brameld, T. B. H., 10
Breckenridge, M. E. and Vincent, E. L., 114, 133
Bridges, K. M. B., 95
Brightbill, C. K., 142
Bronfenbrenner, U., 126
Brouha, L., 18, 20
Brown, H. S. and Mesersmith, L., 65
Bruce, 92
Buber, M., 129, 133
Burnett, I. and Pear, T. H., 60
Buskirk, E. R., Anderson, K. L. and Brozek, J., 29

Cannon, W. B., 76

Carstairs, G. M., 11, 15
Carter, J. E. L., 46
Carter, M., 10, 15
Castle, E. B., 104, 133
Cerf, W., 115
Chace, M., 88
Clarke, H. H., 48
Clarke, L. V., 66
Coelfield, J. R. and McCollum, R. H., 19
Coleman, J. S., 102, 133
Cooley, C. H., 127
Corlett, H., 35
Cowell, C. C., 70, 74, 83, 95, 98, 99, 111, 124, 142
Cozens, F. W., 62, 66
Cozens, F. W. and Stumpf, F. S., 136
Cratty, B. J., 48, 67, 74
Cross, T. J., 63
Crowther Report, 13, 15
Cureton, T. K., 44, 45

Dalzell-Ward, A. J., 48
Davis, E. C. *et al.*, 48
De Cecco, J. P., 74
Decroly, 127
Dennis, W., 23
Dewey, J., 3, 15, 55, 71, 124, 129
Dimock, H. S., 38
Drever, J.,
Drinkwater, D., 109
Durkheim, E., 10
Dyson, G. H. G., 68, 74

Education Policies Commission, 121
Edwards, K. J., 122
Ellis, Havelock, 86, 92
Ellwood, C. A., 126
Elvin, H. L., 15
Espenchade, A., 37, 38, 39, 40, 48
Eysenck, H. J., 1, 15, 43

163

SUBJECT INDEX